Reimagining Library Spaces

Transform Your Space on Any Budget

Diana Rendina

International Society for Technology in Education
PORTLAND, OREGON • ARLINGTON, VIRGINIA

Reimagining Library Spaces
Transform Your Space on Any Budget
Diana Rendina

© 2017 International Society for Technology in Education
World rights reserved. No part of this book may be reproduced or
transmitted in any form or by any means—electronic, mechanical,
photocopying, recording, or by any information storage or retrieval
system—without prior written permission from the publisher. See
www.iste.org/resources/permissions-and-reprints.

Editor: *Emily Reed*
Copy Editor: *Karstin Painter*
Book Design and Production: *Kim McGovern*
Cover Design: *Edwin Ouellette*

Library of Congress Cataloging-in-Publication Data
Names: Rendina, Diana L., author.
Title: Reimagining library spaces : transform your space on any budget /
  Diana Rendina.
Description: First edition. | Portland, Oregon : International Society for
Technology in Education, [2017] | Series: Digital age librarian's series |
  Includes bibliographical references.
Identifiers: LCCN 2017040254 (print) | LCCN 2018022682 (ebook) |
  ISBN 9781564846372 (mobi) | ISBN 9781564846389 (epub) | ISBN
  9781564846396 (pdf) | ISBN 9781564843913 (pbk.)
Subjects: LCSH: School libraries—Planning. | Libraries—Space
  utilization. | School libraries--Information technology. | Educational
  technology—Planning. | Makerspaces in libraries. | School libraries—
  United States—Case studies.
Classification: LCC Z675.S3 (ebook) | LCC Z675.S3 R446 2017 (print) |
  DDC 022--dc23
LC record available at https://lccn.loc.gov/2017040254

First Edition
ISBN: 978-1-56484-391-3
Ebook version available.

Printed in the United States of America.

ISTE® is a registered trademark of the International Society for
Technology in Education.

About ISTE

The International Society for Technology in Education (ISTE) is the premier nonprofit organization serving educators and education leaders committed to empowering connected learners in a connected world. ISTE serves more than 100,000 education stakeholders throughout the world.

ISTE's innovative offerings include the ISTE Conference & Expo, one of the biggest, most comprehensive events in the world—as well as the widely adopted ISTE Standards for learning, teaching and leading in the digital age and a robust suite of professional learning resources, including webinars, online courses, consulting services for schools and districts, books, and peer-reviewed journals and publications. Visit iste.org to learn more.

Join our community of passionate educators

ISTE members get free year-round professional development opportunities and discounts on ISTE resources and conference registration. Membership also connects you to a network of educators who can instantly help with advice and best practices.

Join or renew your ISTE membership today! Visit iste.org/membership or call 800.336.5191.

About the Author

 **Diana Rendina, MLIS,** is the media specialist at Tampa Preparatory School, an independent 6–12 school. Prior to this, she was the media specialist at Stewart Middle Magnet School for seven years, where she transformed their library and piloted their makerspace program. Diana is passionate about school libraries being places for students to discover, learn, grow, create, connect, and collaborate. She is the creator of the blog RenovatedLearning.com and is also a monthly contributor to AASL Knowledge Quest. Diana participates actively in the International Society for Technology in Education Librarians Network, the American Association of School Librarians, and the Florida Association for Media in Education (FAME). She is the winner of the 2016 ISTE Outstanding Young Educator Award, the 2015 ISTE Librarians Network Award, the 2015 AASL Frances Henne Award for Emerging Leaders, and the 2015 School Library Journal Build Something Bold Award. She has presented on the maker movement at state, national, and international conferences. Diana is on social media as @DianaLRendina. She coauthored *Challenge-Based Learning in the School Library Makerspace* with Colleen Graves and Aaron Graves. *Reimagining Library Spaces* is her first single-author book.

Other Titles in the Digital Age Librarian's Series

Connected Librarians: Tap Social Media to Enhance Professional Development and Student Learning by Nikki D Robertson

Inspiring Curiosity: The Librarian's Guide to Inquiry-Based Learning by Colette Cassinelli

Leading from the Library: Help Your School Community Thrive in the Digital Age by Shannon McClintock Miller and William Bass

To see all books available from ISTE, please visit iste.org/resources.

Acknowledgments

This book would not have been possible without the support of so many others who helped me along the way.

Thank you to the students and staff of Stewart Middle Magnet School. The seven years I spent there were some of the most formative of my career, and this book could not have happened without the people willing to support my sometimes crazy ideas. Thank you to the administration for letting me take down shelves, paint walls with whiteboard paint, and mount Lego baseplates onto the walls. And thank you to my students, for never ceasing to amaze me with your ingenuity and creativity.

Thank you to my new Tampa Preparatory School family. I'm excited to see where this next phase of my life takes me.

The librarians, media specialists, and educators that I interviewed for this book helped to make it richer and broader in scope. Thank you to Wendy Lopez, Jessica Malloy, Todd Burleson, and Andy Plemmons. Thank you to my amazing PLN as well, especially Colleen Graves, for commiserating about book writing and editing with me.

Thank you to Valerie Witte and the team at ISTE for being amazing to work with.

And of course, thank you to my family, especially my husband, Giancarlo, who put up with me holing up in a room with my laptop and poring through research to get this book done. I couldn't have done it without you.

Contents

Contents

Introduction

In March 2010, I was fresh out of library school and excited about getting my first "real" job as a media specialist. After interviewing at several schools, I was hired at Stewart Middle Magnet School, a STEM magnet, Title I school in Tampa, Florida, just fifteen minutes from my house. After finishing all the paperwork on my first day there, the reading coach took me on a tour of the school and walked me to the library. He opened the doors to the media center, and I let out a small gasp: it was a dark, dusty, neglected cave.

Half of the lights didn't seem to be turned on, which left the room dim. Shelves lined every inch of available wall space, and they were crammed with musty-looking books. There were large shelving units on the floor as well, packed to the brim. As I walked toward the circulation desk to meet my secretary (whom I would lose to budget cuts the following year), I stumbled around extra desks in the middle of the library. There was stuff everywhere I looked, and I wasn't exactly sure where my desk was supposed to be. There was even an old card catalog in the back room, and an atlas stand holding materials approximately ten years out of date.

In the instructional area, there were ten huge, heavy, wooden tables with tons of chairs. It was impossible to walk through, let alone hold a class. Students sitting in the area had their backpacks on the floor or hanging off the chairs; they barely had enough room to squeeze into their chairs. Because there was no wall space, the only place to use a projector was on pull-down screens that blocked bookshelves. (Not that there were outlets to plug a computer or a projector into in those areas.) The tops of the bookshelves were too high for students to reach; they were cluttered with old projects from the art class (which we also lost the following year to budget cuts). The art projects had a thick layer of dust on them—the students who had made them were long out of middle school.

Figure 0.1. The Stewart Media Center Instructional area circa 2011.

The walls were dull, industrial beige. The carpet was dingy gray and needed thorough shampooing: there was a large coffee stain in one area, probably from a mishap at a faculty meeting. The video storage room was so tight that it was hard to walk around inside, and the shelves were packed with LaserDisks, vinyl records, and VHS tapes on topics such as the Soviet Union and other out-of-date topics that were no longer part of the curriculum.

Library school prepared me for creating a collection development plan and a policies and procedures notebook. It taught me how to deal with censorship challenges, and how to teach information literacy skills. It gave me a wonderful overview of current children's and teen's literature and gave me a chance to learn storytelling and evaluating materials. But I don't think anything could have prepared me for the experience of working in my first school library.

Transitioning the Space

I didn't want to rock the boat too much in my first year, so I made changes slowly. I rearranged some of the existing furniture to improve the flow so that we would stop running into things. I removed the unused teacher desks from the middle of the floor and returned them to the district warehouse. I acquired a desk for myself and set up a place for it on the library floor so I could be present with students. There was a teacher work area in the back, but working in there cut me off from students. The room wasn't ideal for getting work done anyway because it was a pass-through to the teacher restroom.

I began the long process of weeding the collection dramatically. My first criterion was to weed out any books that students hadn't been checked out since 1984 (the year I was born). This ended up being several thousand books! The collection had been in such bad shape before I arrived that it was featured in a local newspaper exposé. I got rid of several giant carts of old, musty books and welcomed new ones. My students were ecstatic that there were now books they actually wanted to read in the library.

It took me several years of weeding to get the collection under control. As I weeded, I shifted books and condensed the collection. I especially tackled reference and biography, which featured up-to-date materials such as biographies of 90s pop stars and Jackie Kennedy giving a tour of the White House. I was able to eliminate several giant floor units. As space opened, I used funds from our bookfair to create a comfy reading nook where the floor units had been. I gradually cleaned up the library, removing the old art projects of past students and replacing them with student-friendly signage to help people find the books they needed. I freed shelf space to create book displays. I got rid of the atlas stand and the card catalog. My students were now checking out books like crazy, but there were still a lot of major flaws in the physical layout of our space.

The Transformation of 2014

The major shift for our library occurred in 2014. That January, I piloted our makerspace by putting three bins of K'NEX building tools on our wooden tables. K'NEX are construction toys made up of rods and sprockets of different sizes, allowing for the fast, easy creation of all sorts of projects (knex.com). My students embraced the concept immediately, and we gradually added new tools and experiences. It became clear that we needed a new type of space for this active learning, so I began meeting with a group of students called the makerspace planning committee to discuss our ideal space.

At this point, anytime I taught a class or hosted an event in the library, our makerspace supplies were put away. My students expressed that they wanted the space to be setup so they could access these materials even when events took place in the library. We talked about how this space would look, what would be in it, how students would use it. As we brainstormed, I worked on DonorsChoose.org projects and grants to fund our ideas, since we had no budget. We started making small changes, such as rearranging our tables and moving our instruction space around. We purchased a small projecting/teaching podium with bookfair funds to free up space when teaching. These experiments helped us plan the bigger changes. I talked with vendors, visited other schools, and looked for inspiration on Pinterest. I shared my findings with my makerspace planning committee and asked for their feedback and ideas.

That summer, we received a Lowes Toolbox for Education Grant for $5,000. We used the money to buy new, flexible tables and chairs for our instruction space, as well as paint to brighten up the library. We got rid of excess shelving and moved a whiteboard from our copy room into our instructional space. Our principal bought us a short-throw projector that we mounted above the new-to-the-space whiteboard, freeing up space in the instructional area. We also removed the wall shelves in the area that became our makerspace.

We had painting parties over the summer and got rid of the old furniture. Then we used DonorsChoose projects to fund a Lego wall and a whiteboard wall to go where some of the wall shelving used to be.

Figure 0.2. Instructional and makerspace area after the transformation.

The 2014–15 school year saw a complete transformation in the physical space of our library and how we used it. Now we could easily accommodate multiple classes with the makerspace still available. Students could use the library for study, play, research, reading, and so on. This library was completely transformed from the dark, dusty cave I walked into in 2010. It took some hard work and elbow grease, but we got there. Check out the Library Profile on Stewart in Chapter 1 to see more before and after pictures.

Transformation Is Possible

I share this story not to intimidate you, but to help you see that YOU can transform your library space. Budgets are strapped everywhere. Librarians are constantly fighting against the stereotypes associated with our spaces and our professions. Some in education, and in society, are questioning whether we need libraries in schools anymore. Transforming our physical spaces to meet the needs of our modern students can help us to show that we are not only relevant but essential to education. In the last few years, I've talked with dozens of school librarians with all sorts of spaces, both new and newly renovated, libraries in historic school buildings, and everything in between. We've shared our stories about searching for funding, discussing our visions with administrators, involving our students in our spaces, and making incremental changes that have huge impacts. I've seen amazing things happen when school librarians are willing to take the risks and the initiative to reimagine their library spaces with their students' success in mind. I hope that you'll take this journey with me and reimagine your space in a way that makes it the best possible library for your students.

Renovated Learning

Throughout this book, I refer to my blog, Renovated Learning (RenovatedLearning.com). I began blogging consistently around the same time that I started my library transformation, and I documented the process, including the development of our makerspace. If you want to see more details of my story, I'd recommend looking there. On my blog, I've also curated resources related to makerspaces and learning space design, many of which I reference in this book. I've added a page specifically focusing on resources related to this book, including links to all of the books cited here. If reading this book makes you eager to dive deeper into learning space design, or leaves you wanting to know more about day-to-day specifics of a transformed library space, make sure you check it out.

Learning Spaces and the ISTE Standards

While it may not seem like it on the surface, there are many ways in which transforming your physical library space can connect to standards and transform student learning. In each chapter, you will find a box discussing how the contents of that chapter relate to one or more of the ISTE Standards for students, educators, and administrators. One of the most relevant standards for this book is ISTE Standards for Students 1b, which states that students "build networks and customize their learning environments in ways that support the learning process." .Throughout this book, I'll be addressing the importance of student voice and student choice in your library space. This will be seen in focusing on flexible, modular furnishings that students can reconfigure easily to suit their needs. It will be seen in creating a variety of learning zones, such as small group areas, large group areas, and quiet study areas. By having a variety of zones available, students can choose the learning environment that works best for them and their tasks at hand.

I'll talk about how you can involve your students in the design process of planning and creating your new space. This ties in beautifully with Standards for Students 4, where students take on the role of the innovative designer: "Students use a variety of technologies within a design process to identify and solve problems by creating new, useful or imaginative solutions." Having your students directly involved in the design process of a new space will be a learning opportunity for them, as they learn how to use design thinking to solve problems in the space.

There are also many Standards for Educators that I'll address throughout the book. Most notably, I'll discuss the changing role of technology in libraries and how we can create a technology-rich learning space for our students in our libraries. This directly relates to Standards for Educators 2a, which states that educators "shape, advance and accelerate a shared vision for empowered learning with technology by engaging stakeholders." By moving beyond the desktop computer lab and making available a wide range of technology and technological experiences in our library space, we will lead the way in our schools by providing our students with opportunities to take control of their learning with technology.

By reading up on the various learning space design theories discussed in Chapter 2, we'll be engaging Standards for Students 5c, which states that teachers "evaluate and reflect on current research and professional practice on a regular basis to make effective use of existing and emerging digital tools and resources in support of student learning." Throughout the rest of the planning process, we'll use this research to help us formulate ideas and advocate for the changes that need to be made to our learning spaces.

Finally, by forming a focus group, surveying our students and community, and involving our community directly in the physical redesign of our spaces, we are meeting ISTE Educator Standard 5b, which states that teachers "exhibit leadership by demonstrating a vision of technology infusion, participating in shared decision making and community building, and developing the leadership and technology skills of others." Our community plays a vital role in our spaces, and by showing leadership through involving them in the process we are helping them to see the library space as their own.

Action Steps

While this book doesn't strictly need to be read in sequential order, most of the chapters build upon the ideas and exercises in the previous ones, so I recommend reading in order the first time you read through this book. At the end of each chapter are several suggested action steps. These are not required, but working through them as you read the book will empower you to see how and where your library space needs transformation. If you work through all the action steps, by the end of this book you will have created a solid plan for your library space and will be ready to approach your administration, school board, or others with your ideas.

CHAPTER 1

The role of school libraries is shifting with the rise of technology in education, digital resources, and the changing learning styles of our students. We must rethink and reimagine our library spaces if we are to remain relevant.

Rethinking Our Spaces

As a child, I fondly remember trips to both my public and school libraries. There were story times and programs, all the picture books I could want, quiet corners for curling up with a book, and the space was decorated with pictures and stuffed animal characters from my favorite books.

There were also stacks of books that towered about me in unreachable rows, a confusing card catalog that I needed a parent or teacher to help me navigate, imposing wooden tables for silent research, and librarians who chided me if I got a little too loud or excited.

While libraries of the past often inspire good memories, our students, our schools, and our libraries are changing. The school library's purpose has grown far beyond that of a repository of books, a research center, and a quiet reading area. The growth of technology in education, the rise of ebooks and online resources, and the changing learning needs and styles of our students all demand that libraries must adapt or become irrelevant. Librarians must rethink and reimagine the physical space of our libraries, and the tools and technology that go into them, if we hope to remain a vital part of our children's education.

Advocating for a New Vision of Libraries

Unfortunately, many teachers, administrators, community members, and even librarians still cling tightly to the libraries of their youth. They see nothing wrong with library spaces filled with large, immovable wood tables with heavy chairs. They see libraries as spaces solely designed for quiet study and reading. Or, by contrast, they are ideal computer labs or testing centers. Worse, libraries are considered multipurpose rooms for schools to host every faculty meeting, parent meeting, and after-school event. Some people even question whether school libraries are necessary at all!

In 2014, one school district in Florida no longer saw the relevance of a school library space staffed with a certified librarian. They eliminated their media specialist positions, rehired many under the new title of Technology Communication Coaches, and dismantled most of their media centers. Some schools moved all the books from the school library into classroom libraries. Others added reading rooms in computer labs, or redesigned their library spaces as multi-purpose meeting rooms. But these spaces lacked a qualified librarian and were being run by secretaries or volunteers (Solocheck, 2014). Some of these transformations were student friendly, but it is disturbing to remove a certified school librarian from the equation, not to mention eliminating students' choices regarding which books to read.

As school librarians, it behooves us to be one step ahead of such changes. We must advocate for updating and transforming our libraries and for our essential roles in these spaces. We must share our vision for how we can transform our library spaces, how libraries are more than relevant—they are vital—in today's schools, and how we play an essential role in the education of our students. It can be exhausting to have to fight tirelessly to prove our worth, but it is necessary in today's world of line-item budgets. Later in the book, you'll read about how Andy Plemmons worked with district committees to plan a brand new library as a part of his school's reconstruction process. Throughout the process, he not only had to advocate for his space but also for the importance of a central, well-equipped school library in a school that was moving in the 1:1 direction. In essence, he was advocating for the role of libraries (and school librarians) as a whole (A. Plemmons, personal communication, February 20, 2017).

Sullivan (2013) states: "Your school library must evolve into a learning environment that supports the educational model of your school and your students." It is now more important than ever for our spaces to change as our schools and pedagogies shift.

Advocating for Updated Spaces

Many who question the relevance of school libraries also have traditional notions of what functions school libraries serve. We must work tirelessly to share what happens in our spaces.

For example, many people have no idea that libraries play a vital role in hosting collaborative teaching lessons, teaching information literacy skills to students, hosting book clubs and other programs. They don't understand that libraries serve as a meeting place for specialists to work one-on-one with students, as well as being a place for students to check out books, read, and study. We must share the many different roles that our space fulfills.

Through this framework, we can address the design problems of our spaces with an understanding of how they impact students and instruction. An administrator might not understand why you need to get rid of large tables and cumbersome chairs until they witness you stumbling over student backpacks while attempting to teach a class, or see a student climbing over chairs to retrieve a book. Your district might not understand why you need more data drops installed in your computer lab until they see how the awkward configurations of computers makes it difficult for students to collaborate on group projects. Your teachers might be frustrated that you want to relocate the copy room to create a reading room until they witness a student who cannot find a quiet place to study while two classes are using the library simultaneously.

Advocating for Our Role

As you saw in the earlier example from Florida, we must not just advocate for changing our spaces, but also advocate for our role within our spaces. You can create a gorgeous, modern library space with lots of natural light, flexible furnishings, and an outstanding collection, but if a full-time librarian does not staff it, it will be much more limited, and students will feel the impact.

Part of advocacy relates to sharing those stories about your space that we talked about earlier. Share about how you co-planned with a new teacher on an upcoming lesson. How you worked with a small group of students by giving them a mini-lesson on database research. How you pulled a variety of novels related to the Holocaust for a unit your language arts classes are studying. There are many misconceptions about what school librarians actually do. Share with your administrators, teachers, and community about what you do on a regular basis.

ISTE STANDARDS CONNECTION

ISTE Standards for Educators 2a: Educators shape, advance and accelerate a shared vision for empowered learning with technology by engaging with education stakeholders.

In advocating for rethinking and reimagining our library spaces, we are sharing our vision for our libraries. Leading with our vision for the ways technology can empower educators in libraries is vital to garnering support for our library space transformations.

The Changing Role of Technology and Libraries

A massive shift in technology use in education has occurred since those days that I spent in my school library as a child. For many years, static desktop computer labs were considered sufficient technological resources for our students. But now, with the affordability of tablets, laptops, smart phones, and other technology advancements, our students are using many other devices besides desktop computers. And many of our schools are making the leap to a BYOD program or a 1:1 setting where every student has their own school-owned device. As librarians, we must embrace and support a diverse variety of technology tools for our students.

Print vs. Digital

Some of you reading this book will be old enough to remember using card catalogs to find resources in the library, others know card catalogs only as awesome garage sale finds made for transforming into stylish coffee tables. A vast amount has changed in libraries in the last thirty years. We can now quickly search our library catalogs on computers. Schools and library systems have created their apps for students and patrons to browse their collections and resources. Our physical reference collections have dwindled with the rise of readily available digital resources and the shorter shelf life of print reference in an ever-changing world.

Digital resources have an impact on the physical spaces of our libraries and need to be addressed here. Libraries benefit from having both physical and digital collections, and they should be balanced. As schools add more ebooks and database subscriptions, the need for an extensive print reference collection lessens. The print collection begins to shift more toward books that students read for pleasure and information, and away from books required for curriculum-related research.

Ebooks

The physical size of our libraries often limits the number of print volumes we can carry. Many students are now bilingual in digital and print literacy. They will often switch back and forth between print books and ebooks. Some will be working on one book on their phone or tablet while also reading a different book in print. Our libraries need to meet this demand by providing diverse ebook collections that can support the needs of our students. These will likely be a blend of fiction and nonfiction. If possible, see if you can develop your ebook collection in collaboration with your school district or with a network of other schools—this can help to lessen costs overall.

Online Databases

Print reference materials have been on the decline for years. Aside from when teachers force them to use print materials, students almost always reach for digital resources first. Unfortunately, many will choose the first article that pops up on Google or Wikipedia. As librarians, we need to be advocates of our online databases. We need to teach students digital research skills and help them work through the various databases we support, such as Gale, World Book, and ProQuest. We need to teach them citation and writing skills. Just because print reference is going away doesn't make our role irrelevant—it makes us more relevant than ever.

The Learning Space Needs of Our Schools

The pedagogies of our teachers and classrooms are shifting. Many schools rely more and more on group work, team projects, and hands-on activities. These styles of work often require a different physical space than the traditional classroom layout. While many schools are transforming the learning space design of their classrooms, the library can also serve as a learning space to meet these needs. Throughout this book, I discuss ways to transform library spaces to be flexible, to support collaboration, and to provide materials and resources for hands-on projects. Even for schools that have redesigned their classrooms, the library is still a vital space because it is available to all students and it houses librarians who can assist students in their work.

Flexibility

With the rise of active learning pedagogy, teachers need access to spaces that can shift and adjust to the needs of students. They need tables that can transform into puppet spaces, or furniture that can move out of the way for a class play: setups that allow small groups to work together comfortably on hands-on projects. In this book, I'll discuss how to create such flexible learning spaces in our libraries, even if we have little to no budget. By creating such spaces in our libraries, we can serve our teachers and students who need a flexible learning space outside of their classrooms. We can also act as a model classroom for our school and encourage further learning space design shifts.

The Third Space

The concept of a third space is one that is outside of work and home. For our students, their "work" space is the classroom. Therefore, our school libraries can serve as that third space for our students; it is an important and unique function of library spaces in schools. Students can come to the space for individual research, whether it's a passion topic of their choosing or an assignment for class. They can come to get away, de-stress, and lose themselves in a book. They can come to hang out with their friends during lunch and play a board game. Or to meet up for a study session for the history test they have next period. These are experiences that our students are unlikely to have anywhere else in the school. Some classroom spaces might support these uses, as might more updated cafeterias. But for the most part, the school library is the one area in the school where students can comfortably "let their hair down" and be themselves. As you advocate for the importance of your role and of updating your space, remember that not all functions of the library need to be strictly or traditionally academic.

📖 LIBRARY PROFILE

SCHOOL: Stewart Middle Magnet School, Tampa, Florida

STAFF: Diana Rendina, media specialist (2010–2017)

GRADES: 6–8

Stewart Middle Magnet School is a 6–8, Title I STEM magnet school. It has an enrollment of eight to nine hundred students. It is a part of the Hillsborough County Public School System, the eighth largest school district in the United States. The main school building, where the library is housed, was built in the 1950s as a segregated African American high school. The current library is located in the room that was once the original school's cafeteria. The district retrofitted the room into a library, with the kitchens turned into office spaces. The large windows in the room were bricked over so that they could install wall shelving for the books.

You read about my first impressions of this school in the introduction. When I first arrived in 2010, it was clear that the library had been neglected for a long time. The collection was horribly out of date. The library was crowded and cluttered with unnecessary, entirely inflexible furniture (see Figures 1.1a and 1.2a). The only place to project while teaching classes was on a screen that pulled down in front of books. The layout of the space was haphazard.

Over the course of several years, I pared the collection. I was able to remove wall shelving and floor shelving units to create space. We got rid of unnecessary furniture and rearranged what was left to improve flow. In 2014, we created the makerspace and received a grant for new tables and chairs (see Figures 1.1b and 1.2b). We painted the walls in blues and greens and created a dedicated presentation space.

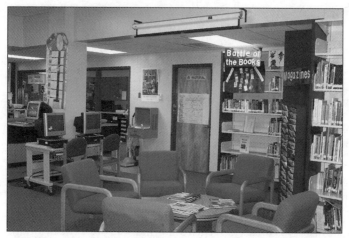

Figure 1.1a. Before: The corner in the Stewart media center circa 2011.

Figure 1.1b. After: The Stewart Makerspace circa 2014.

Figure 1.2a. Before: The instructional area in the Stewart media center circa 2013.

Figure 1.2b. After: The instructional area in 2014, after receiving Lowe's Toolbox for Education Grant.

Now the library is far more flexible than before. The furniture and layout can quickly adapt for different purposes, and checkout is maintained even when classes are in session. You'll read more about Stewart throughout the book.

Action Steps

Document the regular activities of your school libraries.
Take photographs. Write summaries of your day. These will
give you documentation you can use to demonstrate what
functions the library currently serves as you advocate for a
change in your space.

**Look up the digital collection resources available to your
school.** Compare these collections with your print collection
and consider the different roles they serve.

CHAPTER 2

While most learning space design theory tends to focus on the classroom or the entire school, there are many applications to school libraries. Several theories will be examined here, including active learning spaces, Thornburg's ideas, and the learning commons model.

Introduction to Learning Space Design Theory

The field of learning space design theory is fascinating and constantly evolving. Current research revolves around school spaces and classrooms in general. There are books about creating environments that support creativity, spaces that embrace a variety of technological tools, and facilitating student collaboration. Some focus on the architecture of the school, while others examine furniture layouts, colors, and tactile elements. Even though much of this research isn't specifically about library spaces, there is still much to glean from it. In this section, I write up some of my favorite learning space design theories with the strongest applications for library spaces.

Fair warning: this chapter gets a little academic. I want you to gain a little background knowledge in the field of learning space design so you can apply what you learn to your library. Having research to back up your ideas and plans will go a long way in helping you to advocate for your space. Several theories will be examined in this chapter, including active learning spaces, Thornburg's ideas, and the learning commons model (Table 2.1).

TABLE 2.1 | Learning Space Theories Summarized

LEARNING SPACE THEORY	SUMMARY
Active Learning Theory	Focuses on creating a variety of learning spaces that allow students to engage in learning actively. Furnishings that are flexible, ergonomic, and mobile are a must. Spaces should include zones with the six learning spaces of large group areas, small group areas, quiet study areas, community areas, technology-rich zones, and makerspaces.
Thornburg's Learning Metaphors	Learning spaces should include four different zones that reflect how humans live and interact. The zones are *campfires* (whole group instruction), *watering holes* (learning from your peers), *caves* (learning alone), and *life* (learning through hands-on application).
The Learning Commons Model	A library space transformed in a way that includes: a shift in mindset (focused on collaboration), 24/7 access to digital resources through a Virtual Commons, and a flexible learning space that is user-centered. In general, the overall collection size is diminished.

Active Learning Theory

In the book *Get Active: Reimagining Learning Spaces for Student Success,* authors Basye, Grant, Hausman, and Johnston explain the vital importance of creating learning environments that support active learning in our students. They describe active learning as "a practice and philosophy that supports student engagement. It offers students a variety of learning styles and choices so that they can more easily collaborate with one another, nurture their innate curiosity and creativity and ultimately succeed" (2015). The most important elements in an active learning space are supporting student choice, flexibility, and bringing the outside world into the classroom. Some of the impediments to active learning the authors describe are in many of our libraries: "[rooms] that don't support communication and collaboration; chairs too big and heavy for students to move; desks and tables that hinder group work, mentoring, information sharing and content creation" (Basye et al., 2015). Throughout the book, the authors offer suggestions for rethinking and transforming our learning spaces in ways that support active learning. Most of the examples and scenarios focus on classrooms, but they are easily applied to our library spaces.

Flexible Furnishings and Spaces

Flexible learning spaces help students to learn digital age skills, commonly described as the four Cs: communication, collaboration, creativity, and critical thinking. It can be easy to focus solely on the types of furnishings we put in our active learning spaces, but Basye et al. warn that "furniture, on its own, doesn't create an optimal learning environment" (2015). The layout of the space, the environment cultivated by the educators, and the materials available to students all play important roles.

Still, there are many aspects to consider when purchasing or rehabbing furniture that is conducive to an active learning environment. The authors suggest focusing on factors of comfort, ergonomics, flexibility, mobility, and durability (Basye et al., 2015).

Comfort

If a student is uncomfortable, constantly shifting and adjusting, they're unlikely to focus on learning. Not every student will be comfortable on the same type of chair, so aim for a variety of seating options. Multiple height choices are critical (i.e., floor level, standard, café-height, standing). Consider less traditional chairs such as bean bag chairs, yoga balls, and wobbly stools. Student choice is critical in this realm, so as much as possible, allow students to select what type of chair they will use.

Ergonomics

Our students' bodies are growing and changing, yet many school furnishings do little to support their spines and posture. Look for options that include lumbar support and armrests (Basye et al., 2015). Multiple height options and adjustability are also necessary, as you will have a wide variety of student sizes.

Flexibility

Your furnishings should be modular and easy to reset and readjust. Ideally, the furniture should be flexible enough that the students themselves can quickly change and shape the space to suit their needs. Items should be able to serve multiple functions depending on the users' needs.

Mobility

Furniture needs to be light enough to be moved easily. Tables on castors that can fold up are ideal. Chairs should be stackable and light enough to move. Heavier items should be on wheels.

Chairs that swivel or move are also useful. It is OK to have some permanent, stationary items, such as bookcases that create cave spaces.

Durability

Students can be hard on furniture, so it's important to make sure our investments of time and money will last. Look for items designed for the heavy use of a school environment. Surfaces that are easy to clean and care for are ideal. When looking at upholstered furniture, make sure that the design is such that you can eventually reupholster it.

Figure 2.1. A variety of seating options are available in the Stewart Middle Magnet School Media Center.

Flexible Furnishings in Action

When I started transforming the instructional space in the library at Stewart Middle Magnet School, all these factors came into play when choosing new seating. The original chairs were large, wooden, and hefty. They couldn't be stacked, so we had to line them up along the walls. They were hard and lacked padding, which lead to a lot of squirming during class as students tried to get comfortable. When students hung their backpacks on the chairs, they would often fall over and cause a lot of disruption. We replaced these chairs with ergonomic, lightweight plastic chairs. These chairs are stackable, which makes it easier to reconfigure the space. The backs of the chairs are more flexible and have cutouts, so students can fidget or sit backward comfortably. And, because they were designed with a school environment in mind, the chairs are also durable and easy to clean.

In addition to these chairs in the instructional space, there are also Hokki Stools with uneven bases that allow for movement, café-height stools, rocking chairs, and soft couch-like chairs (see Figure 2.1). This variety in seating makes it easy for students to find what works best for them.

ISTE STANDARDS CONNECTION

ISTE Standards for Students 1b. Students build networks and customize their learning environments in ways that support the learning process

By creating a flexible, active learning environment with modular furnishings, librarians empower their students to exercise student voice and customize their learning environment. Students can self-select what chairs, tables or other areas they need for they work they have to complete.

Six Active Learning Spaces

The authors of *Get Active* identify six types of active learning spaces that are essential for creating an engaging learning environment for students: small group areas, large group areas, community areas, technology-rich areas, quiet, solitary areas, and makerspaces (Basye et al., 2015). Libraries are arguably the ideal place in our schools to incorporate all six types of learning spaces in one location. All students have access to the library, and it is naturally a multipurpose, multifunctional space. Libraries are the learning hubs of our schools. You might find that many of these spaces will overlap in your library, or that a space's purpose might shift depending on the day. That's reasonable, considering the necessary flexibility of our spaces. Aim for having all six areas available as much as possible.

Small Group Areas

Collaboration is a vital skill for our students to learn as they prepare for the workforce of the future. In your library, make sure that you have areas available where small groups of students can meet, talk, and brainstorm. For one school, this might be a row of diner booths on one wall. For another, it might be whiteboard tables set up for small group brainstorming sessions. Other schools might have teaming tables with a monitor where students can share their device screens. It's all about what works best for your space and your students. If possible, try to allow for small groups to have a bit of privacy, so they don't feel like the entire library is overhearing their conversations. Provide materials for brainstorming solutions, including mobile whiteboards, whiteboard top tables, and collaborative technology.

This type of space will do more for your students than merely provide a location for group work. You'll likely see groups of students gathering in these areas to socialize, play board games, and eat a snack together. Providing a safe social space for students is an important purpose of the library—not all functions need to be strictly academic.

Large Group Areas

Active learning theory emphasizes the importance of group work, collaboration, and student driven learning. But that doesn't mean that there won't be times when you will need whole class discussions, lectures, and presentations (Basye et al., 2015). By default, most school libraries already have a large group area that can support this style of learning. This area is typically the learning space where you hold classes; it is often quite multifunctional and will serve many different purposes throughout the year. It should be a space where entire classes can comfortably work, move around, and converse.

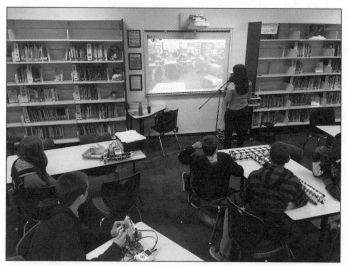

Figure 2.2. A large group area at Stewart Middle Magnet School.

Flexibility and student choice are essential in this area. Advocate for flexible furnishings if you are still stuck with the large, traditional library tables. Having furniture that is reconfigurable in your large group area will make it easier to transition the space for different styles of teaching and learning. Make sure that you have an easy-to-use presentation setup too—ideally, this space should always have a projector, laptop, and screen set up and ready to go. Basye et al. recommend setting up this space to have no set "front of the room;" however, that might not be doable in every library space (2015). If you have the room, create multiple large group areas to accommodate multiple classes and learning styles. Dividing walls and separate classrooms can potentially help with noise issues.

Community Area

Community areas provide a space for presentations, parent meetings, and special events. Often, the community area will also serve as the large group area. Some libraries are lucky enough to have an auditorium or multipurpose room attached. If you aren't, more than likely your large group area will also be where you host special events like author visits, bookfairs, parent meetings, and so on. This is why flexibility is crucial for making your learning space truly active. When advocating for furnishings in this space, be sure to mention the importance of quick and easy transitions for community events.

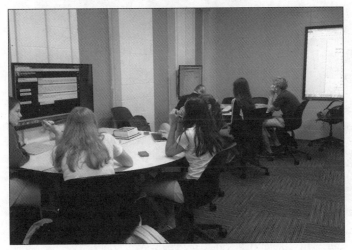

Figure 2.3. The TEAL Lab at Santa Fe Catholic High School in Lakeland, Florida. *Photo by Wendy Lopez.*

Technology-Rich Area

Your library should have a space where students can utilize technology. Many of us have computer labs or stations in our libraries already, but try to think beyond the basic computer lab. Could you include tablets that students can check out? Could you purchase a high-powered computer setup for photo editing? Could you create a small music studio in an old storage room where students could record podcasts, music, and spoken word poetry? Maybe you could use teaming tables to create a TEAL lab (see Figure 2.3, Chapter 3, and Santa Fe Catholic's story at the end of this chapter). With more and more of our students already equipped with their own devices, we need to rethink how we can provide technology experiences that they don't already have. For more ideas on creating a technology-rich area in your library, see Chapter 3.

Figure 2.4. The quiet reading and study room at Santa Fe Catholic High School in Lakeland, Florida. *Photo by Wendy Lopez.*

ISTE STANDARDS CONNECTION

ISTE Standards for Educators 2b. Educators shape, advance and accelerate a shared vision for empowered learning with technology by engaging with education stakeholders.

ISTE Standards for Educators 5a: Educators use technology to create, adapt and personalize learning experiences that foster independent learning and accommodate learner differences and needs.

By creating a flexible, technology-rich learning space, librarians can support student learning and creativity in the library. A virtual learning commons can also help to support student use of digital tools.

Quiet, Solitary Areas

Once upon a time, our libraries were pristinely silent, intended solely for students to come in and read a book quietly. However, that paradigm has shifted, and many of our libraries are now active, vibrant, and—at times—a bit noisy. We still need to serve those students who want a place to lose themselves in a book or dive deep into studying for an exam. Despite the constant push towards group work and collaboration, there is great value in work done in solitude. Many of our students need that quiet space to read, study, research, and reflect independently.

Try to designate a quiet room or quiet zone in your library, where students will know to keep the volume down. Later in this chapter, you'll read about the Santa Fe Learning Commons. When the school renovated this space, clear dividing walls were added to create a small room attached to the main room of the library (see Figure 2.4). This room is now the quiet reading and study area, where students know they can go to cram for a test or curl up with a good book (W. Lopez, personal communication, February 10, 2017). Look into creating "cave" spaces by rearranging furniture (such as bookshelves) or providing screens or dividers to help students find solitude (more on caves in the next section on Thornburg's theories). Base et al. recommend creating a three-walled space that allows for monitoring of students while creating a sense of privacy (2015). Try to arrange your space so that students will have a minimal amount of interruptions.

Figure 2.5. The Stewart Middle Magnet School makerspace.

Makerspaces

Makerspaces come in all shapes and sizes, from a bin of Legos on a table in the corner to a full-blown fabrication lab with 3-D printers and laser cutters. How exactly it comes together in your space depends on what works best for you and your students. Try to find a way to give students access to hands-on materials with which they can explore new ideas and have creative play experiences. This might be a Lego wall, a whiteboard wall, or an arts-and-crafts supply cart. Whatever it is, make sure you have a place for creativity in your library.

Thornburg's Learning Space Metaphors

David Thornburg is a futurist, author, and consultant whose work focuses on the relationship between learning space design and student learning. He is also the head of the Thornburg Center, which focuses on emerging technologies and the impact that they have on learning. In his book, *From the Campfire to the Holodeck,* Thornburg explains his four primordial learning metaphors (campfire, watering hole, cave, and life) and how they apply to our modern learning spaces (2014). The discussion focuses primarily on classrooms, but all four of these metaphors play a huge part in school library spaces as well.

Campfires

The campfire is a "home to storytelling—a place where people gather to hear stories told by others" (Thornburg, 2014). In our school context, this is the traditional classroom space where teachers give lectures, students give presentations, and an audience (the class) sits and listens. The campfire is the most traditional of spaces and is overused in many school environments, but it serves a purpose; we shouldn't eliminate it entirely. Ideally, a lecture should only be a part of a lesson, giving "just enough information to set the stage for student discovery" (Thornburg, 2014).

In our libraries, the campfire is the space where we conduct instruction with whole classes. Some libraries have an attached classroom to serve this purpose, and others have an instructional space set up in the main room. Whatever the circumstance, try to set up the space so it can transition from the campfire into a small group space. Be sure to include tools for presenting, such as a laptop, projector, screen, whiteboard, and so on.

Watering Holes

The watering hole is a place for "social learning among peers." Pedagogically, it links to the social constructivism of Vygotsky (Thornburg, 2014). This type of learning occurs in all generations: think of the water cooler, the teacher lounge, the comfortable chairs outside of a conference workshop where participants discuss what they've learned over coffee. Students need this kind of environment to discuss and process their learning with one another.

In a library environment, include spaces for spontaneous student meetings. Comfortable soft seating, portable dry-erase boards, and café-height tables make for excellent student meeting spaces. When teaching large group lessons, be sure to include time for conversation after the lecture. Thornburg notes that after a lecture "learners are engaged in thinking about what they just saw and heard and most naturally, they want to discuss this with others who attended the same event" (Thornburg, 2014). By providing watering hole spaces for students, we are showing them that they have a place in our libraries to engage in conversation.

Caves

Caves are spaces for reflective learning, spaces that are "solitary and involv[e] self-directed meaning making that can be facilitated with outside resources" (Thornburg, 2014). These link with the cognitive constructivism of Piaget (Thornburg, 2014). Cave spaces recognize the fact that learning is personal, and that students need areas where they can avoid interruption.

Figure 2.6. A cave space created by rearranging bookshelves at Stewart Middle Magnet School.

In our libraries, caves could be reading nooks, diner booths, or other small spaces designed for only one or two students. Ideally, these spaces should be semi-enclosed in a quieter area of the library, allowing for the student to have a sense of privacy. If you have it available, a quiet room that is attached to the central area of the library can serve this purpose well (see Figure 2.4).

Life

Thornburg's fourth, and most recent, metaphor is that of life. In life, students can engage in the "meaningful application of the things learned" (Thornburg, 2014). This space connects with Seymour Papert's constructionism, a pedagogy that focuses on learning through making things and tinkering (Thornburg, 2014). Life spaces give students the freedom to explore, experiment, and pursue a variety of projects independently.

In our library spaces, makerspaces are most often the embodiment of life. Makerspaces should provide a wide range of materials and tools to students for tinkering. Thornburg points out that, "the key is that the space can adapt to a wide variety of uses and can be shaped by educational purposes as well as the students' creative goals" (Thornburg, 2014). It is more about providing an opportunity for creative, hands-on open exploration and less about having every student work on the same project at the same time.

Figure 2.7. The Collaborative Classroom in the Santa Fe Catholic High School Learning Commons in Lakeland, Florida. *Photo by Wendy Lopez.*

The Learning Commons Model

The history of the learning commons model is deep and varied. Many trace it to the information commons model that first started appearing in higher education environments in the 1990s (Diggs 2015). By 2008, Loertscher, Koechlin, and Rosenfeld had published the first edition of *The New Learning Commons: Where Learners Win! Reinventing School Libraries and Computer Labs.* It was around this time that the term "learning commons" was gaining traction in K–12 environments (Diggs, 2015).

The exact definition of learning commons varies from one source to the next (much like the ever-changing definition of a school library). Pioneers of the movement define them as "a learning laboratory that is the foundation of all learning in the school rather than a warehouse of information and technologies. The new learning commons focuses on client-centered programs pushing world-class excellence throughout the school" (Loertscher, Koechlin, & Zwaan, 2008). Kompar defines them as a program "inclusive of a rich, integrated, digital and media literacy curriculum; 24/7 access to collaborative media engaging the users in participatory digital spaces and flexible, user-centered creative spaces" (2015). No matter what definition you consider, there are some common themes. In general, a learning commons includes mindset changes, physical changes, and a virtual learning dimension.

Learning Commons Mindset

The shift in mindset that happens in the learning commons model is one that is seen in many school libraries today, regardless of whether they call themselves a learning commons. The mindset shift is a crucial aspect of implementing a learning commons—one can change up the furniture and create a virtual learning space, but if the mindset and perception about the library remain the same, little will change.

In the 2015 Horizon Report, the authors stated that, "the image of a library as an impervious vault wherein librarians serve as the gatekeepers, guiding patrons through myriad stacks, had become outdated" (Diggs, 2015). In a learning commons mindset, this image is shattered. A learning commons space focuses on building "the collaborative learning community necessary to design and sustain the best possible teaching and learning environments" (Loertscher et al., 2008). The concept of collaboration among students and among teachers is critical. Kompar describes a learning commons as a place for students to "think, design, collaborate, inquire, share, solve problems, and develop skills as independent learners and innovator" (2015).

This mindset is radically different from the traditional view of a library as a storehouse of knowledge to be consumed. Thankfully, it's not so different from many school library spaces today that recognize the importance of collaborative learning, innovation, and creativity. When it comes down to it, many schools choose to change the name of their spaces to learning commons because it helps to clarify that a significant mindset shift has happened. Of course, spaces can absolutely embrace these concepts and still call themselves libraries.

Physical Changes

One of the more well-known aspects of a learning commons is the transformation of the physical space. You've likely seen images of school libraries transformed into learning commons that have bright, beautiful colors and flexible furniture. These types of spaces are much like the active learning spaces and the learning metaphors discussed earlier in this chapter; there's often overlap among different learning space theories.

A learning commons is characterized by "flexible, user-centered creative physical spaces" (Kompar, 2015). The furnishings and layouts are designed to support and encourage collaboration. It also supports creating a comfortable environment where students can "work, relax, learn, create or do" (Loertscher et al., 2008).

When Valerie Diggs, department head of school libraries for the Chelmsford Public Schools, transformed her library into a learning commons in 2008, she surveyed her community, worked with a renovation committee to come up with a report, and then met with library facility consultants to come up with a floor plan. She collaborated with a design-savvy colleague to decide on carpet tiles, shelving, and furniture. They brought in sample chairs for students and teachers to "comfort" test. She made changes to the physical space: removing cement walls, weeding 10,000 books, adding low shelving to let in more light, and adding student-friendly furniture such as café-height tables and restaurant-style booths (2015).

Virtual Learning Commons

The final aspect of the learning commons model involves creating a virtual learning commons space that is accessible to students 24/7. Learning isn't confined to the school day—it's happening before and after as well, and a learning commons can support that with a virtual space that students can use (Loertscher et al., 2008). This virtual space could include database access, links to resources and Web 2.0 technologies, a social media presence, discussion boards for students, and so on. For more on creating such a space, check out the books *The Virtual Learning Commons* (2012), by Loertscher, Koechlin, and Rosenfeld and *The Whole School Library Learning Commons: An Educator's Guide* (2016) by Judith Anne Sykes.

 LIBRARY PROFILE

> **SCHOOL:** Santa Fe Catholic High School, Lakeland, Florida
>
> **STAFF:** Wendy Lopez
>
> **GRADES:** 9–12

The Santa Fe Catholic High School library transformed into a learning commons over the summer of 2014. It was a small space, crammed with books on every bit of available wall space. The library was one large room, and it was hard to accommodate multiple classes and small groups.

The transformation included adding glass walls to create separated learning spaces, heavily weeding the collection, and replacing the furniture. The current space has several distinct zones: the quiet reading room (Figure 2.4), the TEAL Lab (Figure 2.3), the collaborative classroom (Figure 2.7), and the broadcast studio.

Figure 2.8a. Before: The Santa Fe Catholic High School Learning Commons before renovations. *Photo courtesy of Wendy Lopez.*

Figure 2.8b. After: The Santa Fe Catholic High School Learning Commons after renovations. *Photo by Wendy Lopez.*

The school has an excellent collection of online resources and ebooks; instruction on how to access and use these resources is part of the curriculum. The school decided to reduce the collection size dramatically and focus on books for pleasure reading. These materials are available in the quiet reading room, which is a glass-walled room with bookshelves, comfortable chairs, and tables to work. This room functions as a study room, but it is also a semi-private location for specialists to meet one-on-one with students.

The TEAL Lab is a collaborative computer lab that includes six teaming tables with monitors, all covered with whiteboard tops. There is a teacher instruction area in the front, and the glass walls enclosing the room can be written on with dry-erase markers. I'll talk more about the TEAL Lab in Chapter 3.

The collaborative classroom is the instructional space. It includes a Smart Board and projector setup for instruction. The tables are small, lightweight, and modular, which makes it easy for students to reconfigure the space. The chairs are lightweight and stackable. This space also includes a mobile whiteboard cart, which allows for student brainstorming and collaboration.

The broadcast room includes a green screen, video equipment, and an iMac. It's used to create the school's morning show, and the equipment is available to the general student body for digital projects.

Santa Fe's Learning Commons is a vibrant, active space, frequently used by multiple groups of students and classes at the same time. Despite its small size, it is the learning hub of the school (W. Lopez, personal communication, February 10, 2017).

Action Steps

Identify the different types of active learning spaces present in your library. Does your library have all six types of active learning spaces yet? If not, what are some actions you can take to create those missing spaces?

Ask, where are the four primordial learning metaphors present in your space? Do students have opportunities to engage in multiple metaphors during your lessons?

Ask, what does your library space have in common with the learning commons model? Are there aspects of this theory that could be woven into your space?

CHAPTER 3

Technology has become an essential part of today's educational environment, and this must be reflected in our school libraries. This chapter will address various ways that our libraries can support and enhance student technology use.

Technology in Modern School Library Spaces

Technology has become a vital and essential part of modern education. For our school libraries to remain relevant, we must support the technology use of our students and teachers. We should be the digital hubs of our schools. Initially, this took the shape of having a traditional computer lab. However, this too is shifting, and we must remain aware of the current changes in educational technology. We must also advocate for the funds and resources necessary to support our schools.

Computer Labs

Computer labs have been a part of school libraries for the past twenty or thirty years. We must consider (and reconsider) how desktop computer labs and laptop computer labs fit in with an educational system that is becoming more connected than ever, especially in BYOD and 1:1 schools.

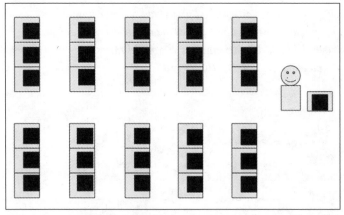

Figure 3.1 Traditional computer lab layout, where computers are situated in rows and the instructor has a station to monitor students.

The Traditional Computer Lab

A traditional school computer lab has between twenty and thirty computers, enough so each child in a full class can have their own device. Schools often organize these labs into rows. Sometimes the computers surround the perimeter of a room, especially if the computer lab is in a separate room from the main library. Some traditional labs have teaching stations set up with a projector, screen, and teacher computer. Other labs simply have an instructor station with software so the teacher can observe what is happening on each student's computer. These types of labs tend to be geared more towards "drill and kill" exercises, online modules, writing, research, and so on. They usually do not accommodate collaboration or group work very well because there is no room for groups of students to work around one computer. Their setup is not conducive to student presentations, either. These types of computer labs are common in school libraries, and they work very well for computer-based standardized testing, which often leads to library closures during testing.

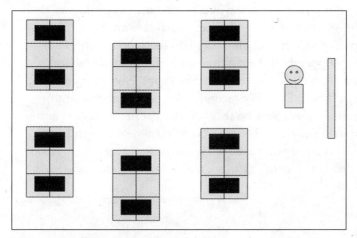

Figure 3.2 Collaborative computer lab layout, where computers are grouped in clusters.

Collaborative Computer Labs

In contrast to a traditional computer lab, a collaborative lab may have fewer than thirty computers, or it may have enough for a full class. Instead of rows, these labs arrange the computers in clusters or similar configurations. There may be additional space on the desk surrounding each machine to accommodate notebooks, paper, or smaller devices. Collaborative labs have a presentation setup that works well for both teacher instruction and student presentations. This type of computer lab setup fits in well with a modern school library. By supporting collaboration, student presentations, and teacher instruction, a collaborative computer lab changes the way we use technology. This type of lab probably wouldn't work well for students going through "drill and kill" exercises, but for collaborative group projects, research, and class presentations, a lab like this can shine.

There are two factors to note with this style of computer lab. First, it is possible that it will take up more physical space than a traditional computer lab. Traditional labs are designed for efficiency, whereas collaborative labs focus on collaboration and group work. If the required amount of physical space becomes an issue, you might need to have fewer computers than in a traditional lab. The second factor is that administrators sometimes push back on this lab style because it doesn't accommodate standardized testing as well. If necessary, cardboard dividers can be purchased or created, allowing students to take tests without being able to see their peers' screens.

Figure 3.3 The Santa Fe Learning Commons TEAL Lab.

TEAL Lab

TEAL stands for Technology Enabled Active Learning. In this style of computer lab, there are no desktops. Rather, tables with monitors are provided, along with connectors that allow students to use laptops, tablets, or other devices—these are called teaming tables. (I will address teaming tables in more detail in the following section.) In the Santa Fe Learning Commons in Lakeland, Florida, their TEAL lab consists of six teaming tables. Each of these tables has a whiteboard top for brainstorming and collaboration. The tables are modular and on castors, thus they can be easily rearranged. Each table has a large monitor that can connect to student devices and a wireless keyboard for typing and entering data. Teachers can display their laptop or tablet on each screen, or select a student's screen to display. There is also a Smart Board mounted in the front of the classroom for the teacher to use for instruction. The flexibility and technological richness of this space allow for more active, collaborative lessons. It wouldn't work for traditional individual computer work or "drill- and-kill" exercises. But there's probably already another computer lab in the school for that.

Desktops vs. Laptops

The debate between using desktop and laptop computers in the school library can be heated. There are numerous pros and cons to both sides, so you must consider many factors when deciding which will work best for your library. Here are some questions to ask yourself:

- How important are portability and mobility? Is my library space set up for students to move around, or is it preferable to have students work in one area?

- How frequently will the computers be used? Will they be turned on and off throughout the day?

- Do space limitations necessitate being able to use the computer lab area for other functions?

- What amount of wear and tear can we expect?

- How secure is the library computer lab area? Is the door locked at night? Is the library used after hours?

- Are these computers going to be used for standardized testing?

- How reliable is the Wi-Fi? Will computers need to be hardwired into the internet at times?

- Do students need to be able to save their work on a flash drive, or does the school utilize cloud storage?

- How many outlets are available? If using laptops, how will they be charged?

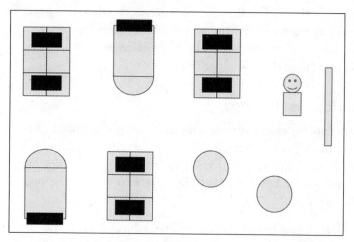

Figure 3.4 Model of a hybrid collaborative computer lab, which mixes computer clusters with teaming tables and tall tables for laptop work.

There is not necessarily one perfect solution. Ultimately, it is about discovering what will work best for your library and your students. Ideally, if you have space and funding, offer students a combination of laptops and desktops so you can accommodate a variety of projects and learning styles.

Hybrid Collaborative Labs

A hybrid collaborative computer lab is a lab that combines clusters of desktops with other technology stations, such as teaming tables, open desks for laptops and tablets, or high-tech digital stations (see following section). A hybrid lab is not necessarily designed for an entire class to be doing the same thing at the same time. Rather, it aims to support multiple learning modalities and projects simultaneously.

A hybrid collaborative lab could be a stand-alone space, or it could be a complement to a more traditional computer lab also located in the library. Ideally, you want to provide a diverse selection of learning experiences and tools that can be used by individuals, small groups, and whole classes.

High-Tech Digital Stations

Since the level of technology our students own is increasing, there is less and less need for them to come to the library to use a desktop or a laptop. Especially in BYOD and 1:1 schools, there is often little need for a standard computer lab. A service our libraries can offer to students in such environments is a combination of high-tech digital stations that supply technology and software that is often cost-prohibitive for students to purchase.

Figure 3.5 Recording studio in the John F. Germany Public Library in Tampa, Florida.

Audio Recording Studio

Podcasts are increasingly popular among students, and many teachers harness this passion by allowing students to create recorded podcasts for projects. Many students also have a passion for music and want to record their songs. Audio recording equipment and software can be excellent tools for students in your library. Consider converting an unused closet or office space into a mini audio recording studio. It doesn't need to be state-of-the-art—just an iMac with GarageBand and a few microphones can be used to create quality recordings. Even if you don't have a separate room available, you can create an audio recording and editing station in your library. Make sure to offer instruction through lunch-and-learns or class collaborations on how to use the software. Also, consider harnessing some student "geniuses" to help you learn the technology and teach it to other students—you're likely to find at least a few passionate audiophiles.

Video Editing Studio

Editing videos and making movies are also increasingly popular in the classroom. While anyone can record a video on a smartphone now, it is still advantageous to have quality software for editing. Consider investing in a computer with software such as iMovie or Final Cut Pro. Make sure to include sound-canceling headphones as well.

If you have a morning show studio in your library, consider ways to make this technology available to your students throughout the day. Perhaps you can create a system to sign up for this space, or you can collaborate with a class on a video project and teach students how to use the morning show equipment in the process. It seems a shame to have such technology in your space available to only a select group of students for one hour each day.

Photography Editing/Graphic Design Studio

Software such as Adobe Photoshop and Illustrator can be very cost prohibitive for students to purchase on their own. Load up at least one desktop computer in your library with this software, and make it available to students. Purchase an extra large monitor to make it easier for students to see the details of their work. Also, consider buying a digital drawing tablet. You'll find that many budding artists and designers will be very appreciative of a setup like this.

ISTE STANDARDS CONNECTION

ISTE Standards for Students 2b. Teachers develop technology-enriched learning environments that enable all students to pursue their individual curiosities and become active participants in setting their own educational goals, managing their own learning, and assessing their own progress.

Technology in our libraries is far richer than just desktop computer labs. We can and should use a variety of tools and devices to create a technology-enriched learning environment in our libraries. By offering a rich and diverse selection of technology resources, we can empower our students to take ownership of their learning.

Supporting BYOD and 1:1

With the increased affordability of mobile devices, more and more of our students now bring their internet-connected devices to school. While some schools have banned or restricted the use of such devices, many have embraced them as learning tools as a part of the BYOD movement. In BYOD schools, students have vast resources at their fingertips. They can quickly find the answers to simple questions using Google and Wikipedia. They can find video tutorials on YouTube, or quickly look up the next sequel in their favorite series. It is important for us to find ways to support the productive, educational use of electronic devices in our libraries.

Moving beyond BYOD, many schools have opted to support student learning by ensuring that every student has a dedicated, school-owned (or student-owned), internet-connected device. These 1:1 schools provide one device per student and offer the same device across grade levels (and sometimes across the entire school). Sometimes the devices are tablets such as iPads; other schools offer Chromebooks or laptops. These 1:1 initiatives create both challenges and opportunities for school librarians. They often render the traditional computer lab irrelevant, but they also create fantastic opportunities for collaboration and working with teachers and students on lessons and research.

Depending on what brand of device the school uses, librarians may have to adapt to a new set of tools and resources. Schools with 1:1 iPads must learn what apps are available and approved to create learning experiences. Librarians working with 1:1 Chromebooks must familiarize themselves with Google's G Suite for Education and the resources provided there, while Microsoft districts have to become familiar with OneDrive and Office 365. There may be a bit of a learning curve, but it is vital for school librarians to become proficient in the system that their school district has chosen. Consider pursuing certification in whichever system your school or district selects so you can become the go-to resource at your school.

We need to design our libraries in such a way that they support both student-owned and school-owned mobile devices. These tools can be powerful learning devices if we help our students to use them effectively. The following are ways that we can support mobile devices and incorporate them into our library programs.

Charging Stations

I can't tell you how many times I've watched students (and adults) hunt all over a library for a place to charge their phone. Many libraries, even those built in recent years, often have a laughably small number of outlets. Those with plenty of outlets don't always have them available in safe or convenient places. Most of the outlets at Stewart Middle Magnet School are located below the bottom shelf of the stacks. I used to see students crawling underneath the shelves or sitting on the floor just to find a place to charge their phones.

Following are some ways to make dedicated charging stations available to your students and teachers. Make sure that you have signage near the area to remind students about being responsible for their own devices. Unfortunately, theft happens, and students need to be aware that they are expected to keep track of their own devices.

DIY Charging Stations

A basic charging station is easy to create yourself with a little ingenuity. A simple power strip and some charging cables can work wonders. I recommend looking for a power strip with built-in USB ports—this makes it easier to setup and gives you fewer pieces to monitor. Purchase charging cables for a variety of phones—there are many different styles of charging cables out there, and students will be very disappointed if there aren't any for their phones.

When I created my first DIY charging station, I left all the cables out in the open. They disappeared in about a week. I recommend building a box or finding a container that can keep students from being able to unplug and take cables. You can also store the charging cables behind the checkout desk and have students check them out like other library equipment—just bear in mind that this may exclude students who, for one reason or another, don't want to ask someone for help.

Readymade Charging Stations

Readymade charging stations can be expensive, but they are worthwhile investments for your library space. Some stations can be wall mounted, some are free standing. Many charging stations will allow you to upload your own graphics, customizing your space and allowing you to brand your library.

Charging lockers are another great option for libraries. They tend to be more expensive and take up more space, but students and teachers love them for the added security they offer. Many models allow students to set a combination when they lock their device. You can often purchase these modularly, so if your budget doesn't allow for as many as you would like now, you can add a few every year. If your school has moved to BYOD or 1:1, consider applying for a grant to add charging lockers to your library.

Figure 3.6 Wall-mounted charging station at Stewart Middle Magnet School.

Teaming Tables

When students look closely at tiny screens on tablets, laptops, and phones to create projects for class and conduct research, it can cause eyestrain. If students are working collaboratively in groups, it can be difficult to crowd around one small screen. An excellent solution to this problem is a teaming table. Teaming tables come in many shapes and sizes; in general, they are one, long table with a large-screen monitor and a technology hub with cables that allow different devices to display their screens on the monitor. Some teaming tables enable students to toggle among the various devices on the monitor. Other tables allow teachers to project their device to students or to display a particular student's device to the entire class. (See the TEAL lab section earlier in this chapter to see an example of a teaming table setup.) This technology significantly increases the collaborative possibilities in a BYOD school.

If your school doesn't have the space or desire to create a TEAL lab, it's still worthwhile to consider adding one or two teaming tables to your library. As student device use continues to grow, having a teaming table will support your students and allow them to use their own devices in collaborative and productive ways.

Mobile Devices and the Blended Library

Since you are allowing students to use electronic devices in their library, why not create a library environment that is interactive with technology? There are many different apps and tools that we can use to blend mobile device use into our library programs. The following are just a few ways that you can encourage mobile device use and blend technology into your library.

QR Codes

QR codes are computer-generated images, usually made up of squares. A mobile device can scan these codes with a QR reader app. Once scanned, the device will be directed to a website, image, or video, or given a piece of text. Adding QR codes to physical objects throughout your library is a simple and effective way to communicate information to your students.

There are endless possibilities for incorporating this technology into your library space. I've listed a few options below.

> **Create book display signage with QR codes that link to book trailers about the items on display.** Display signage is a straightforward and easy option to create. When you assemble a book display on a particular theme, look up video trailers for the book on YouTube or a similar video-sharing site. Create a QR code to the link, and use a photo editor to add the code to your display signage.

HOW TO CREATE A QR CODE

QR codes can work for internet links, text, images, etc. This tutorial will focus on links, but the same idea applies to other QR codes as well.

1. Find the item you want to link to and copy the web address.

2. Go to a QR code generator, such as QRstuff.com, and paste in your link.

3. Download a jpeg image of your new QR code.

This picture can be imported into a program like Microsoft Word or Canva. You can use it as a part of your library website, or you can print it out and post it in your library. The possibilities are endless!

Create stand-ins for your ebooks that will connect the student's device to your ebook checkout system. Stand-ins for ebooks can be set up using old VHS cases. Use a photo editor to upload a color image of the book, and add a QR code linking your ebooks to the picture. Print this out and attach it to an old VHS case, then shelve it in the stacks.

Create virtual displays of students' digital work. Upload images of your students' digital work (with their permission) to a photo-sharing site such as Flickr. (Or use a different hosting site, such as SoundCloud for audio, YouTube for video, etc.) Create a graphic that includes the student's name, the title of the work, a brief description, and a QR code linking to the student work. Print these out on cardstock and set up a gallery in your library. Make sure that they are displayed at eye level so students can scan them.

Create a QR code scavenger hunt. QR codes work for text as well as links. Use this feature to create QR codes that offer students clues as to where the next code will be hidden. Have them solve the clues and continue finding and scanning the remaining QR codes. A QR scavenger hunt can be a fun activity to host in your library.

Augmented Reality

Augmented reality (AR) is a new and growing technology that has lots of potential for school libraries. By using an augmented reality app, images, text, and other information are superimposed on the screen of a device. By using a variety of augmented reality apps, school librarians can add a new dimension of hands-on, technological learning into their library spaces. Here are some potential applications:

Augmented Reality Book Displays: By scanning the cover of a book, a student can link to a book trailer, or a video of a fellow student's book review might pop up.

Augmented Reality Nonfiction: Many publishers are beginning to add AR into their books. Now, instead of merely looking at a figure of a human heart, students are able to scan the page and manipulate a 3-D image of a heart.

Augmented Reality Library Orientations: For your next library orientation, consider dividing students into groups, handing them a device, and sending them out to different corners of the library. Students can "scan" particular parts of the library, such as the circulation desk, computer lab, and so on, and get information and videos about the policies surrounding those areas.

Makerspace Technology

Makerspaces are one of the six active learning spaces we discussed in the previous chapter (Basye et al., 2015). They are also the embodiment of Thornburg's primordial learning metaphor of life (2014). I've been writing about makerspaces since I started the makerspace at Stewart Middle Magnet School in 2014. The scope of makerspaces as a whole is much greater than this book. For this chapter, we'll take a look at the role technology plays in makerspaces, and how this can bring a greater technological richness to your library space.

Tech vs. Non-Tech Makerspaces

One common misconception about makerspaces is that they solely focus on technology. There is a common idea out there that you must have a 3-D printer to have a makerspace. While 3-D technology is excellent, it is not true that makerspaces require technology. Amazing, hands-on learning experiences can happen in a makerspace with—or without—technology. At Stewart, students had amazing learning experiences designing furniture in Tinkercad and printing out their designs on the 3-D printer. But they also had fantastic experiences building models out of cardboard, glue, paint, and recycled supplies.

Make sure that you don't write off non-tech experiences for students in your makerspace. Many low- and no-tech tools are complemented by technology and also enjoyed on their own. For example, students love to create designs with Perler beads, tiny plastic beads that students arrange on pegboards. The beads are then melted together using wax paper and an iron. While this activity is no-tech, students will spend time on Pinterest or Google browsing for images of projects to create. They'll use pixel-generating tools to create templates for their designs, and they'll take pictures of their creations and share them on social media. So while the activity itself is no-tech, students still utilize technology throughout the design process.

Makerspace Technology Activities

There are a plethora of options out there for makerspace technologies, and the list is growing every day. When deciding what types of technology you want to include in your makerspace, don't just go out and buy one of everything on this list. Look at your school and curriculum—are there classes that already use some of this technology? Could you complement that in your makerspace? Where do your students' interests lie? (We'll learn more about that when we do our surveys and focus groups in the next chapter). Are there tools that can work with the technology your school already has, such as iPads or Chromebooks?

Here are some possible makerspace technology activities to consider for your library space:

Coding

You actually don't need to buy anything new for this one because you already have what you need—a computer! Code. org is a great place to start, and there are tons of websites available for students to learn how to code. You can also consider purchasing technology that can be coded, such as Arduino (a programmable microcontroller) and Raspberry Pi (a minicomputer). Many robots and circuit kits also have coding capabilities.

Robotics

Robots can be super fun, and there are more and more options coming out every day. In addition to being entertaining, there are all sorts of math and science connections (as well as other subjects) that can be incorporated with robots. Students can learn about calculating angles by programming Sphero (a spherical robot) to go through a maze. They can build their physics knowledge by building an obstacle course for Lego Mindstorms. And, of course, there are endless opportunities to learn more about computer science and programming by coding robots to perform specific tasks. Many robots require an iPad or similar device to control them, and you can program many with third-party apps. Look into robots such as Sphero, Dash and Dot, Lego Mindstorms, and Ozobots.

Circuits

Understanding how circuits work can expose students to a whole new world of electrical engineering—no soldering iron needed (although you can certainly have those in your maker-space, too). Consider kits like littleBits and Snap Circuits for a great intro for students. Or look into activities like sewable circuits and paper circuits, so students can design projects they can take home.

3-D Modeling

You don't have to have a 3-D printer for students to learn about 3-D design. However, 3-D printers are quickly becoming more and more affordable, so they're likely to become more common in school libraries. Students can use programs such as Tinkercad and Blokify to create their own 3-D designs. Programs like these are a great step toward spurring student interest in computer-aided design (CAD).

Action Steps

Look at the computer lab in your library. Ask, which of the models does it fit? Could you change this space in a way that would allow for more collaboration?

Get certified. Explore earning certification in whichever platform or system your school/district uses (Google Certified Educator, Apple Teacher, Microsoft Certification, etc.).

Create a DIY charging station. Buy a power strip (preferably with built-in USB ports) and some charging cables.

Download a QR reader and/or an augmented reality app. Create a book display that uses one of these technologies, and encourage students to try it out with their devices.

CHAPTER 4

*Before we can transform our library spaces, we need first to take a good,
hard look at what we've got to work with. It's vital to spend some time
analyzing the physical space, observing how students and teachers use
the space, and surveying your school community to identify their needs.*

Taking Stock of Your Library Space

As we prepare to transform and reimagine our library
spaces, it is crucial to take stock of our spaces. Even the
most out-of-date, poorly designed school library has
elements that work for students. There are easy changes
that we can implement once we take the time to observe
how our current space works and evaluate the resources
that are already available to us.

Taking stock of your library space will take some time,
but the process is worth it. If we immediately jump into
making changes without thinking things through, we can
make costly decisions that waste funds and create environments that don't support or welcome our students. It will
be much harder to get stakeholder buy-in after making
such mistakes.

Taking stock of your space involves three elements: inventorying your space, surveying your community, and forming a library design team. When inventorying the space, we take a look at what's already there and see what things we've been overlooking. Surveying your community through both question-and-answer surveys and a focus group will help you gain a better idea of the needs and interests of your users. A library design team will help in using design thinking to process the information you've collected and brainstorm workable solutions.

Inventorying Your Physical Space

The first step is to take an inventory of the physical space of our libraries. This process requires a bit of time and effort, but it's well worth it to gain some perspective into how your library currently functions. The inventory will help you to identify strengths and weaknesses in your library space. It will also help you to find areas to focus on as you work to transform the space. There may be elements of your space of which you were unaware. If you've been in your library space for a long time, this step is especially relevant because your familiarity with how the space has been used can make it more difficult to imagine fresh layouts or unusual arrangements that you might otherwise have visualized.

Create a Layout Diagram

Interior designers and architects often start their design and redesign of a space by creating a layout diagram of the area. We don't necessarily need to break out the drafting table to accomplish this—there are many easy solutions for creating diagrams of our library spaces. You don't need to be an architect or be proficient in CAD to do this. Even a simple sketch on paper, or a doodle in Microsoft Paint, can help us to plan. That said, if you're working with an architect or a vendor, they are often more than happy to create a professional diagram of your space for you, often free of charge.

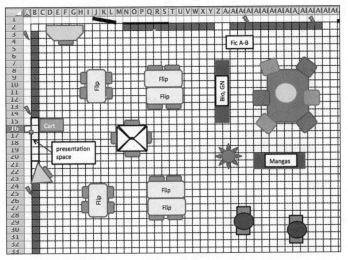

Figure 4.1 Excel layout diagram sketch of Stewart Middle Magnet School media center in 2016.

A to-scale diagram of your space helps you to get a better idea of how the room flows and what you can change. If you create pieces to represent your furniture (e.g., shapes in Excel or paper cutouts), then you can rearrange and rethink your space without physically moving a single piece of furniture. Creating a layout diagram can be as complex or simple as you like. The main idea is to get a feel for your space and how everything works together.

For a detailed tutorial on how to create a layout diagram in Microsoft Excel, refer to the following feature on creating a layout diagram in Excel," adapted from my blog post titled, "How to Create a Floor Plan in Excel" (renovatedlearning. com/2016/08/29/floorplan-space-excel). Visit the post to watch a YouTube tutorial that demonstrates each of the steps. You can also download a copy of the Stewart media center Excel layout, which you can use as a starting template for your own.

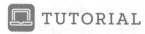 TUTORIAL

Creating a Layout Diagram in Excel

1. **Create a rough draft on graph paper (or sketch it out on regular paper).**
   This step might seem counterintuitive, but it's easier to sketch out your floor plan on graph paper first, and then take that information to make a spreadsheet. Grab a tape measure, and measure the boundaries of the room(s) for which you're creating the floor plans (make sure to take notes as you go). If you have access to the blueprints, use those. Using one square on the graph paper to represent one square foot, draw out the basic boundaries of the space. Now it's time to put the stuff in your space.

2. **Measure ALL THE THINGS!**
   Measure the length and width of every table, desk, chair, storage unit, etc., in your space. Write down the measurements on a notecard. For now, you don't need to worry about exactly where they fall in the area. What you DO need is a list of how many of each item you have and their sizes (e.g., six 30″×60″ tables, four 36″×90″ bookshelves, etc.). Don't worry about the height—that isn't a factor in this spreadsheet. Once you've got all the data written down, it's time to transfer that to the computer.

3. **Set up your spreadsheet like a grid.**
   Excel spreadsheets start out with wide columns, which doesn't work well for floor plans. I like to create a grid of

squares where each square represents one square foot. That makes it the easiest for planning out the space. Select all of your columns and adjust their widths until they look close to perfect squares. You can test this by creating a square and seeing if it fits correctly in a row and column when you rotate it, but if that sounds complicated, don't stress out—it doesn't have to be perfect.

4. **Create the boundaries of your space in Excel.**
   Count out the boundaries of your space based on your scale, and highlight those squares. Create a bold border around this area to help you see the scale you have. Note: If your room isn't rectangular, this might be tricky. Remember, your diagram doesn't have to be perfect, so just do the best you can.

5. **Create fixed objects.**
   If individual elements of your space are fixed in one place, such as wall mounted library shelves or a circulation desk, add them straight to the grid. For the shelves at Stewart, I highlighted the areas where they are located and colored those squares burgundy. This step helps me to get a visual idea of where they are, and it'll be useful in the next step when creating furniture items.

6. **Set up and arrange your furniture items.**
   Using the measurements you took earlier, create the furniture pieces of your space. Your furniture icons can be as simple or complex as you like. Basic rectangle shapes tend to work best for most things. I like to color code my shapes in colors similar to the furniture items because it helps me to remember what they are. Try to position the objects relatively as they are now.

7. **Group items as needed.**
   If there's a certain grouping of furniture that always goes together (e.g., chairs at computer tables), you can group the items together using the group function in Excel. Hold down Control (PC) or Command (Mac) and select each of the items you want to group. Then choose "group items." Now, when you move one, you can move all of them.

8. **Play house.**
   Now that you have all your furniture elements in place, save your file. Then Save As and create a new file for experimentation and ideas. Move your furniture and experiment with new layouts. Create shapes for furniture items you're thinking about purchasing, and play around with your space. This process is my favorite part of creating an Excel layout—it makes it so easy to experiment with new ideas.

Reproduced from www.renovatedlearning.com

Observe Your Space Like an Anthropologist

When anthropologists want to study a new culture or society, they spend time observing the locals. They watch for customs, gestures. They look at how different people interact with one another and their surroundings. In the same way, we can be anthropologists in our libraries by observing our students.

Take a look at your library space with fresh eyes. Watch how students utilize the space. Take notes of the traffic flow patterns. Spend a good amount of time really noticing how different groups of students use the various areas of the library. This observation might be difficult for you at first, but as you start to see how students physically interact with the space, you'll start noticing changes that need to happen.

One useful guideline is the AEIOU acronym created by Conifer Research and described in-depth by Margaret Sullivan in *Library Spaces for 21st Century Learners: A Planning Guide for Creating New School Library Concepts* (Sullivan, 2013). The book is a fantastic resource for the practical aspects of planning and funding a space transformation, and I highly recommend it. The letters in AEIOU stand for: Activities, Environments, Interactions, Objects, and Users.

Activities

Look at the various activities your students are engaging in, including researching on the computer, reading a book, socializing with friends. Where students move, how they rearrange the furniture, the amount of lighting they have, and what posture they take are all things to note.

Environments

Look at other spaces that students use outside of schools, such as museums, stores, and amusement parks. More on finding inspiration from spaces like these appears in Chapter 5.

Interactions

Observe how your users interact with the space and each other. Consider the tactile elements of the space, comfort, noise, conversation levels, and so on. Look at how students interact and work with one another. Does the current space support or hinder interactions?

Objects

Notice any objects that a student uses. These can be anything from basic school supplies (a student taking notes with pen and paper), using computers or tablets, to the different types of chairs they prefer to use for certain tasks.

Users

Observe your students themselves. Striking up informal conversations with your students and asking casual questions can help you to gain a wealth of insight (Sullivan, 2013).

In the extraordinary book *Make Space: How to Set the Stage for Creative Collaboration,* Doorley and Witthoft (2012) recommend taking the time to observe the way that your users (students) manipulate your space. By watching for these "user-initiated changes," you can discover hacks and modifications that can improve your space for students. Look for things that students are using unconventionally or surprisingly. At one point in the transformation process at Stewart, I had pushed some of our heavy tables to the side of the library to create space for a student presentation. Later that day, I noticed a student lying down underneath the table and working on a project (see Figure 4.2). Seeing this helped me to understand that: (1) my students like having places where they can lie down on the floor, and (2) my students enjoy having semi-enclosed cave spaces for reading and working.

Get a Fresh Perspective on Your Space

Ask trusted local colleagues to visit your library space during school hours. Have them spend time observing the students. Physically walk through the room together. Ask lots of questions about their observations. You might want to introduce the AEIOU framework to them, or you can just discover what their natural observations are. The experiences your colleagues bring from their own schools can help you to gain more ideas about how to transform your space.

Figure 4.2 Seeing a student working under a table at Stewart helped me understand the need for cave spaces.

Additionally, consider having someone who works outside of education visit the space. We become so accustomed to how our spaces are set up that we take many things for granted. Having the perspective of someone who doesn't spend forty hours a week in a school library space can provide fantastic insight. Make sure to emphasize that you are looking for honest, candid opinions and observations, and that they should not worry about hurting your feelings. You want the best information possible, not what they think you want to hear.

Surveying Your Community

The purpose of the school library is not to serve as a beautiful book repository, nor is the objective to fit the ideal desires of the school librarian. The school library exists to serve its community—the students, teachers, parents, and other people who visit and utilize the resources and physical space. When reimagining our library spaces, we want to be sure to include the voice of our community early in the process. This can be done best through utilizing a survey questionnaire and creating a focus group.

Creating a Survey Questionnaire

When you're rethinking and redesigning your library, it's vital to make sure you hear the voices of students and teachers in the process. There may be unmet needs in your student body and teaching staff of which you are completely unaware. Sullivan (2013) gives some excellent, detailed instructions and advice for creating a survey and selecting a representative population of students.

You can create a pen and paper survey, if that's what works best for you and your population, but many schools prefer to use a digital tool like Google Forms, Nearpod, or Survey Monkey, as these make it easier to collect and aggregate data. I suggest creating the survey digitally and keeping it to ten questions or less. Otherwise, students might not complete it. Include a variety of question formats, such as yes/no, multiple choice, all that apply, and so on. A few open-ended questions can provide interesting information as well—just bear in mind that it takes a lot more time to sort through the responses. Ideally, there should be only one or two open-ended questions—you should save the rest for your focus group, which we'll discuss in the next section.

Here are some examples of some types of questions to ask:

- Why do you usually come to the library?
  - Study
  - Hangout
  - Check out books
  - Use computers

- What describes your internet access situation at home?
  - Wired internet access
  - Wi-Fi
  - No internet access
- Which of the following technology items do you own? Check all that apply.
  - Smartphone
  - Desktop computer
  - Laptop computer
  - Tablet
  - Other internet-accessible device (Kindle, Nintendo DS, etc.)
- What are your favorite colors to wear? If you could paint your room any color, what would it be?
- Do you prefer to study in noisy environments or quiet environments? Do you like listening to music when you study? If so, what kind?
- What is one thing about the library that you would change to make it better?
- What is your favorite place in the library?
  - Computer lab
  - Comfy chairs
  - Study tables
  - Makerspace
  - Other
- What do you like to do to give your brain a break while studying?

Creating a Focus Group

A survey of your school community will provide with a great deal of invaluable feedback. But there is also much to learn from having real-time conversations with students and teachers about your library space. Gather a focus group and meet with them to plan your transformation. You might have just one meeting, or you might have several separate meetings, depending on the number of participants and what works best for your structure.

Students, Teachers, Parents

Ideally, you will want to have a focus group that is representative of your population. Students from each grade level should be present, as well as students from the ethnic groups and socioeconomic statuses represented in your school. They don't necessarily need to be avid readers or library regulars—we want our space transformation to serve the needs of all our students— not just those who are already coming regularly.

Teachers and parents should be included in the process as well. They can be mixed in with the student focus group, or can comprise a separate group. Look to represent a variety of subject areas, grade levels, and teaching styles for your teachers. With parents, try to get a broad sampling of school involvement—you don't want it to include only your PTSA regulars. However, beware of those teachers and parents who struggle with change—they might shut down ideas for the rest of your focus group with their resistance. Their voices should be heard, but you need to strive for balance, openness, and honesty.

Sullivan recommends having an assistant to record notes, leaving you free to ask more questions and listen intently. If possible, the meetings should be recorded, with signed consent forms from all involved. Be sure to explain that the information will be shared only in aggregate, and that the individual opinions of those involved will not be disclosed (Sullivan, 2013).

Discussion Ideas for Your Focus Group

Begin by having your group brainstorm about the strengths and weaknesses of the library. Give each student some Post-It notes and Sharpies, and have them add their ideas to brainstorming boards. Give them some time to get their thoughts out before you gather the group to discuss them. Look for themes among their observations. Ask leading questions to get more detail.

Here are some examples of good open-ended questions you can ask your focus group:

- What makes the library important to the school?

- What is the first thing you notice when you enter this library?

- When you think of the word *library*, what are some of the first words that come to mind?

- What are some types of activities that you would like to see in the library?

- What are your favorite places to hang out in your free time? What is it about them that makes you happy?

- What is your ideal study environment?

- If you could decorate and design your dream room, what would it look like?

Sullivan has a fantastic list of even more open-ended questions in her book, as well as more advice and strategies for working with focus groups (Sullivan, 2013).

ISTE STANDARDS CONNECTION

ISTE Standards for Educators 4d. Educators demonstrate cultural competency when communicating with students, parents and colleagues and interact with them as co-collaborators in student learning.

ISTE Standards for Educators 2a. Educators shape, advance and accelerate a shared vision for empowered learning with technology by engaging with education stakeholders.

By surveying our community and focus group, and by forming a library design team, we are developing a vision for our libraries and communication by engaging with parents, students, colleagues, and other stakeholders in our schools.

Forming a Library Design Team

Most school librarians are on their own in their spaces, but when planning a redesign of your space, it's good to have a team to help you. This group is your library design team that will work with you to take all the ideas and information you have gathered and translate them into action. There may be some crossover between your focus group and your library design team, but they have two distinct purposes.

The individuals who participate on your library design team will be varied. When I was planning the makerspace and the library transformation at Stewart, I gathered a group of interested students to help me. I also met with my administration to discuss ideas. When Todd Burleson was redesigning the library at Hubbard Woods in Illinois, several parents joined his library design team and visited other schools with him to gather ideas and inspiration (more on Todd's story in Chapter 6).

For your library design team, consider students, teachers, administrators, and parents. If your school is working with architects or designers, include them in the process as well. The Third Teacher +, a design and architecture group focused on reimagining school spaces, recommends considering friends and colleagues who have a good sense of design, especially if you feel unsure about your own (Bill, 2013). You might have separate student and adult teams, or you might have everyone meet together. An advantage to having different groups is that students might feel more comfortable sharing their ideas and input without adults present. An advantage of having them together is that the adults can get a better sense of student needs and interests, and students can see that the adults care about what they think. Create this group in a way that works best for you and your school community.

ISTE STANDARDS CONNECTION

ISTE Standards for Students 4a: Students know and use a deliberate design process for generating ideas, testing theories, creating innovative artifacts or solving authentic problems.

By forming a library design team that includes students and student input, our students are working through the design process to plan, test, and create their library environment. They are also working to solve the authentic problems of the current library space.

Processing Survey and Focus Group Results

For your first meeting, gather your survey and focus group(s) results. Package the information into an easy-to-read report, and send it out to everyone in the library design team before the meeting. As with the focus groups, it's ideal to have someone outside of the team available to take notes and/or to record the session. After everyone has had a chance to review the results, gather your team for a solution session.

In Edutopia's fantastic video series, Remake Your Classroom, designers from The Third Teacher + have their volunteer team brainstorm ideas based around the themes of display, storage, furniture, teaching zone, and personality (Bill, 2013). Your themes might be slightly different based upon your space, but they could include things such as display, shelving, technology, interactive spaces, furniture, instruction space, teaching zone, reading zone, and personality. Consider using tools such as Post-It notes, poster board, whiteboards, and graph paper to organize your design team's brainstorming ideas. The goal is to translate the results of your survey into concrete, actionable plans. We'll discuss more design thinking strategies that you can use with your library design team in next section.

Another option to consider is to brainstorm based on zones of your library. Doorley and Witthoft (2012) created a design template of spaces that focus several zones. They include home base (the main location of individual and group work), gathering spaces (places where people meet in large or small groups), thresholds/transitions (entries, exits, and passages of a space), and support structure (things that support work, such as supply areas, printer/copier, kitchen space, etc.). You can also consider using the types of spaces discussed in Chapter 2, such as the six active learning spaces or Thornburg's primordial metaphors, or create your own names for different zones. Again, always look for what will work best for you and your school.

Using Design Thinking

Education emphasizes design thinking as a mindset and tool for students to use in project-based learning, but it is also a fantastic tool for rethinking and redesigning a library space. By utilizing the information you have gathered, and sharing it with your library design team, you can use design thinking to come up with concrete solutions and improvements for your space.

According to Spencer and Juliani, design thinking is "a way to think about creative work. It starts with empathy, working to really understand the problems people are facing before attempting to create solutions" (2016, p. 24). They also describe it as "a way of solving problems that encourages positive risk-taking and creativity" (2016, p. 52). The key to design thinking is to empathize with whom you're trying to help and come up with a multitude of possible solutions to their problem. Since you've gone over the survey and focus group results with your library design team, they've already started to get a feel for the students and teachers who use the library, and hopefully they have begun to develop empathy and find problems in your space that need solving. Now, have students select a particular problem, brain-storm a variety of solutions for that problem, create prototypes of their solutions, and test them out in your library.

Figure 4.3. Student-designed 3-D printed models for makerspace furniture.

At Stewart Middle Magnet School, our afterschool Stewart makers club used design thinking to create designs for makerspace furniture. The challenge was for them to build designs for libraries that want to start a makerspace and need a little help getting organized. My students did research online, interviewed other students about what problems they encounter in our makerspace, and developed prototypes for their furniture ideas (see Figure 4.3). At the end of the project, students presented their prototypes to an educational furniture representative from Custom Educational Furnishings to get ideas and feedback. One of the students' creations was developed into a makerspace storage cart by the company and was named by the students.

DESIGN THINKING RESOURCES

Books

Doorley, S., & Witthoft, S. (2012). *Make space: How to set the stage for creative collaboration.* Hoboken, N.J.: J. Wiley.

Kelley, T., & Kelley, D. (2015). *Creative confidence: Unleashing the creative potential within us all.* London: William Collins.

Spencer, J., & Juliani, A. J. (2016). *LAUNCH: Using design thinking to boost creativity and bring out the maker in every student.* San Diego, CA: Dave Burgess Consulting, Inc.

Online Resources

Design Thinking For Educators: designthinkingforeducators.com

Design Thinking for Libraries: designthinkingforlibraries.com

The Stanford d.school K–12 Lab Network dschool.stanford.edu/programs/k12-lab-network

If you're interested in learning more about design thinking, check out some of the resources in the box Many of these resources contain sample exercises that you can work through with your students to help them learn how to use design thinking.

Tying Mission into Your Space

As you are brainstorming and processing ideas with your library design team, be sure to take time to discuss both your library mission statement and your school and district mission statements. How does the plan that is forming for your space tie into these mission statements? Work to create some concrete connections, as this will help as you advocate for funding and change.

Sullivan (2013) offers up several excellent examples of ways that the mission can be visible in the library space. For example, if parent and community involvement is an important part of your school vision, consider how your space can be set up to accommodate and welcome parents—maybe you can have a community resources area or a place where parents can read with their young children. If your mission statement focuses on leadership and student responsibility, look at how you can design your library for self-directed, independent use, such as creating student lounges, self-checkout stations, and wayfinding signage. If your school places emphasis on project-based and lifelong learning, consider the establishment of a makerspace and student project area.

Action Steps

Create a layout diagram of your space using Excel, graph paper, or another tool. Spend some time observing your space and take notes. Get an outside perspective from a friend or colleague.

Get input through a survey. Create and send out a survey to your students and teachers to find out their thoughts on your library space as well as what types of environments they like to study in. Use a variety of formats. and promote it in as many venues as possible, so as to get a broad, representative sample of your students.

Form a focus group. Meet with your group of students, teachers, and parents to get more input.

Create your library design team. Hold your first meeting to process the data you received and brainstorm on how to transform it into actionable data.

CHAPTER 5

There are many sources of ideas and inspiration to consider consider as we transform and reimagine our library spaces. Physical institutions focused on education can provide fantastic material with which to work. Internet resources like Pinterest and Twitter offer an even greater amount of inspiration.

Finding Inspiration for Your Space

When reimagining our library spaces, we don't want to limit ourselves to the preconceived notions of how a school library *should* look. We need to get outside of the box, stretch our imaginations, and visualize how our space would look when it was truly serving our students.

There are many places to find design inspiration for your library—physical, print, and virtual. I've found amazing ideas online and in design books, museums, public libraries, and so on. Finding inspiration comes down to keeping your mind open and learning to detect how different types of spaces make you *feel*. Such a method might sound a bit wishy-washy, but eventually, you will start to get a good idea of things to do.

Visiting Other Spaces for Inspiration

Visiting other locations in person is a fantastic way to gain ideas and inspiration for your library space. When thinking about places to visit, don't limit yourself to visiting only other school libraries. There's inspiration to be found everywhere, from public art to traditional education institutions. Consider taking field trips to some of these types of spaces with your library design team, as Todd Burleson did with several parents from Hubbard Woods School (more on Todd's story in Chapter 6). The following are several types of places where I've gotten great ideas.

Figure 5.1 The children's section of the Seattle Public Library.

Public Libraries

Public libraries are excellent sources of library design inspiration. Even though they don't always serve the same range of patrons or support the same programs as school libraries, there are far more commonalities than differences. Public libraries often have more funding for renovations and improvements than do schools, and many large public libraries have innovative and forward-thinking designs. While we might not have the budget (yet) to accomplish such renovations in our spaces, we can still get ideas for changes to make and dreams to aspire to.

Public libraries often have excellent signage and good branding strategies. They're designed to be used by patrons independently. In the same way, we can get ideas for creating wayfinding signage to help our students navigate our libraries. We can see the power of branding and how using consistent colors and fonts in our signage can create a clear mood in our space.

Make sure to visit the children's and teen's sections (see Figure 5.1); public libraries are often on the cutting edge of what works well for these age groups. They often have kid-friendly furnishings, story time areas, technology labs, and other settings ripe for ideas and inspiration.

Figure 5.2 The Learning Commons at the University of South Florida.

Take some time to talk to some of the librarians. Ask them about how their space functions. What would they like to change? What is their favorite part of their space? These answers can be wonderfully insightful.

Academic Libraries

Colleges and universities might not seem like the best place to get ideas for elementary and secondary schools, but again, there are plenty of lessons to be gained. Academic libraries tend to focus heavily on collaboration among students. They also excel in finding ways to keep student devices charged since nearly every college student has a laptop and smartphone nowadays.

In academic libraries, I've been inspired by learning commons/ information commons areas (see Figure 5.2). In these spaces, you'll often see tons of mobile whiteboards, and glass panels mounted to the walls for more dry-erase brainstorming. They tend to include outlets galore and plenty of teaming tables for digital collaboration. One more thing that makes academic libraries student-friendly: snacks and drinks are readily available, and there are designated areas where students are welcome to consume them. Some college libraries even have a Starbucks or similar coffee shop incorporated into their space.

Consider ways that you can create collaborative brainstorming areas for your students. Think about ways to encourage device use by offering places where students can recharge their devices. If possible, consider relaxing your food and drink policies. Maybe designate a "café" area of the library for students to consume food and beverages. If you're in a high school, think about getting a Keurig. Students who are awake are more likely to learn and remember.

Figure 5.3 A makerspace area in the Columbus Museum of Art.

Museums

Museums are designed for informal education, so these spaces naturally provide amazing ideas for rethinking our library spaces. Look for inspiration in art museums, children's museums, science museums, and more. Museums are great resources for interactive spaces and displays. Look at group learning areas and observe patrons interacting with one another; think about ways that you could replicate these concepts within your school.

Many museums encourage a sort of audience participation with their exhibits. At the Columbus Museum of Art (see Figure 5.3), several of the works have space next to the art where patrons can add their thoughts and impressions on Post-It notes. In another exhibit in the museum, patrons can view the blueprints for the newest museum wing, read a statement from the architect about how play influenced his design, and then build their own designs using building blocks. There are many ways in which you could incorporate this kind of interactivity in a school library. You could create a space for students to make book recommendations using Post-It notes. Students could answer a poll on a whiteboard or chalkboard wall. You could create a combination book-and-maker display by asking students to create designs (with Legos, craft supplies, etc.) inspired by the books on display. You could then display these works alongside the books.

For more inspiration on creating interactive, museum-like spaces, check out the book *The Participatory Museum* (2010), by Nina Simon.

Classrooms (and Other School Spaces)

Whenever I visit another school, the first place I want to visit is the library. But sometimes, there are also amazing learning spaces in other parts of the school. Visit innovative classrooms, common areas, lounges, and other creative spaces. When the design of a school is innovative and forward-thinking, every space can be an inspiration.

Seek out a variety of schools and school spaces to visit. Regardless of the grade level, there are ideas to be found in all schools: elementary and secondary, public, private, and charter, urban or rural, large or small.

Public and Private Makerspaces

Makerspaces outside of schools are learning environments often geared toward adults, but that doesn't mean the ideas can't work for the younger set. Look at how they organize their workspaces, how they provide power, how they create access to resources, and how members can store in-progress projects. What elements do they use to inspire ideas? There's a plethora of inspiration you can find in makerspaces, even if you don't have a makerspace in your library yet.

To find local makerspaces, try Googling the name of your city and "makerspace," "hackerspace," or "fab lab." Also, check directories like those found on Make.com. Many of the people who run makerspaces (whether for profit or nonprofit) are very passionate about what they do and are eager to share with others. They can become fantastic partners for you as you reimagine your library space.

Innovative Company Offices

Many startups and technology companies have embraced creative, innovative environments for their workforce. Google and Facebook are famous for their employee cafés, comfortable, homelike spaces and a variety of learning and working environments. Our budgets are certainly not as large as these companies, but that doesn't mean that we can't take from their ideas.

If you're lucky enough to live in, or able to travel to, a city that includes companies with innovative office spaces, schedule a tour. Ask lots of questions about how employees use the space, and take lots of pictures. If you aren't able to visit in person, look up spaces like this on Pinterest (more on this later).

For more inspiration, check out the books *I Wish I Worked There!: A Look Inside the Most Creative Spaces in Business* (2010) by Kursty Groves and Will Knight and *Change Your Space, Change Your Culture: How Engaging Workspaces Lead to Transformation and Growth* (2014) by Miller, Casey, and Konchar.

Other Spaces

Be on the lookout for inspiration everywhere. Artists, designers, engineers, and other creatives often cite finding ideas and inspiration at the most unexpected moments. Be aware of your surroundings while walking through the neighborhood. Watch children playing at a playground. Observe a group reading together in a bookstore. Even consider the layout of your favorite place to shop in the mall, paying particular attention to how it's set up for its customers. Any place, anywhere can provide library design inspiration. You just look for it.

Sullivan recommends visiting spaces that your students frequent. Stores that your students visit, such as The Apple Store, can give you insight into things like lighting and merchandising (2013). If you aren't sure where your students like to hang out in their free time, ask them!

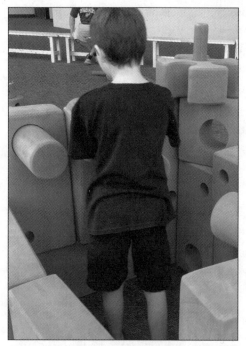

Figure 5.4 The Imagination Playground at the Museum of Science and Industry in Tampa, Florida.

I've gotten ideas from visiting spaces like the Imagination Playground (see Figure 5.4), which consists of giant foam building blocks that students use to build all sorts of creations. I found an amazing piece of street art in Philadelphia made with chalkboard paint and sentence prompts like "I believe ..." and "I wish ..." I've found inspiration in cozy reading nooks in local bookstores. You can find ideas anywhere.

Finding Digital Inspiration

Visiting a variety of learning spaces is an excellent way to get fantastic ideas for your library. Unfortunately, not all of us live near well-designed museums, classrooms, libraries, and maker-spaces, nor are we always able to travel. But no matter where you live, you can access an endless treasure trove of ideas and inspiration on the internet. It may take a little searching and digging to find what you're looking for, but it'll be well worth it.

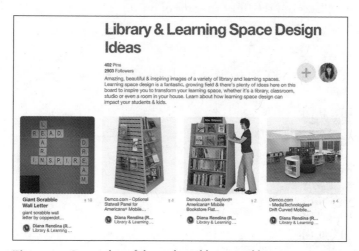

Figure 5.5 Screenshot of the author's library and learning space design Pinterest board.

Pinterest: A Learning Space Design Goldmine

If you've never used Pinterest to find professional resources, you've got to check it out. Pinterest is far more than just the recipes and DIY projects for which it's known. Pinterest functions like a virtual bulletin board. It allows you to browse "pins," which are images and links from websites. You can then pin these to your "boards," creating themed boards filled with inspiration. I've got boards for library display ideas, makerspace organization tips, learning space design, as well as many additional topics. Try searching for a subject that interests you, and see what comes up.

Pinterest is a fantastic resource for learning space design ideas. Browsing Pinterest allows you to "visit" places that you might never be able to see otherwise. You can check out places like public libraries and museums, innovative school spaces in other countries, and more. I've gotten *so* many ideas from Pinterest, including the original inspiration for the epic Lego wall in my library. Check out the links to some of my Pinterest boards below to get started!

PINTEREST BOARDS FOR INSPIRATION

 Library Display Ideas

 Makerspace Organization Tips

 Learning Space Design Ideas

Twitter

Twitter is a goldmine of ideas and inspiration if you know where to find them. The hashtag #libdesignchat is focused specifically on library design—it's a great way to find and share ideas. Also, many school library organizations host Twitter chats, and library design is often a topic of conversation. You can also use popular hashtags, such as #tlchat (teacher librarian chat), #tlelem (elementary teacher-librarians), #makerspace and #makered for ideas about makerspace design, and #edtechchat (educational technology chat) for ideas related to technology in education. These hashtags provide a lot of great ideas. Also, consider asking a question of the group using one of these hashtags—educators on Twitter are happy to share what's working in their schools. The hashtag for this book is #reimaginelib, so that's another great place to find and share ideas from what you're learning in this book.

ISTE STANDARDS CONNECTION

ISTE Standards for Educators 1. Educators continually improve their practice by learning from and with others and exploring proven and promising practices that leverage technology to improve student learning

By seeking out a variety of resources, research, and information, we can get ideas to transform our spaces and support student learning. This allows us to continually improve our practice as we rethink our spaces. Utilizing digital tools, such as Pinterest and Twitter, is a way to leverage technology.

Build a Mood Board for Your Library

In fashion and interior design, many designers begin by creating a mood board of colors, textures, images, and other aspects to inspire them as they come up with their ideas. These mood boards can be created on bulletin boards, on poster boards, or created digitally. As teacher librarians, we too can create mood boards to help inspire us as we reimagine our libraries. I keep my mood board as a bulletin board mounted next to my desk in the library (see Figure 5.6). I look at it every day, and it reminds me of the space and environment I aspire to create in my library.

Collecting Your Inspiration

Start by collecting everything that inspires you. Depending on whether you are creating your mood board digitally or physically, you can scan copies of cutouts you find in catalogs and other print materials or print out color pictures of images you find on the internet. I like to go through this process with physical images because it helps me to get the big picture and see everything with which I'm working.

Your inspiration might come from the items you pinned earlier, or they might come from photos you took when you visited other learning spaces. Look through catalogs for library furnishings, and cut out images of furniture and layouts that you love. Go to a home supply store and gather paint samples of color possibilities for your space. Consider tactile elements as well—maybe a particular type of texture for furniture, a Lego baseplate or whiteboard surface, or even a leaf of a houseplant you'd love to see in your library. During this phase, don't hold back. Add everything that inspires you to your collection.

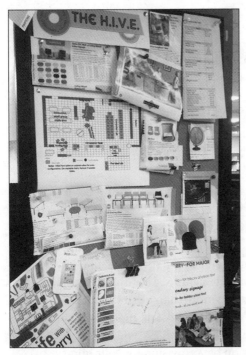

Figure 5.6 One of the author's inspiration boards for the Stewart Middle Magnet School library.

Look to books on design, architecture, and art for inspiration. These don't necessarily have to be books featuring school spaces, but they certainly can be. You might find a beautiful layout in a book on mid-century interior design, a color scheme that you love in a minimalist painting, or an inspiring office space in an architectural journal. One fantastic book for library space eye candy is *The L!brary Book* (2010) by Anooradha Iyer Siddiqi. It covers an initiative started by the Robin Hood Foundation in collaboration with New York City schools and various architecture firms. It features the renovation stories of fifty-one schools in New York City, and the color photographs are stunning.

Editing Your Collection

Now that you have all your inspiration laid out in front of you, it's time to edit and curate. Eliminate any items that are no longer speaking to you or won't benefit your students. Make it a collaborative process—have your library design team work with you to create a cohesive vision for your library space. You don't have to toss these ideas permanently—keep them in a separate folder and revisit them later to see if your thoughts have changed.

Organizing and Looking for Trends

Now that your inspiration is curated, it's time to organize and search for patterns. Lay out your images on your board. Arrange and rearrange them until you love what you see. Look for trends, such as certain colors and elements (e.g., sunlight, plants). If certain images speak to you more than others, print out a larger version of the image or resize it to take up more room on your board. When you finish with this process, you will have a beautiful, visual representation of your vision for your library space. These ideas may not be identically re-created in your library, but they will continue to inspire you as you figure out the practical changes that are possible.

Your Dream Library

After creating your mood board, visiting other learning spaces, and seeking inspiration and ideas online, you will develop a better grasp of how you want your dream library to look. Spend some time fleshing out your ideas. Write a narrative of a typical day in your dream library. Create a mission and vision statement for your dream library. Even if your ideas seem impossible now, I encourage you to spend some time clarifying and writing them out. People respond to passion and plans. When it's clear that you have a passion for what you want your space to be. and a plan for how to get it there, funding and resources may follow.

Design Your Dream Layout

In Chapter 4, you used Excel, graph paper, or another tool to create a layout diagram of your space. Take that same diagram now and either save a copy, create a photocopy, or start from scratch. In this new diagram, forget about everything that is currently in your space. Ask yourself how your dream layout would look. Is there a wall or two that you would eliminate, or shelving units you would remove? Is there new furniture you would love to see? Would you like to add a new doorway to an outdoor courtyard?

Using the original template, create your dream layout. The only rule (for now) is considering the current physical parameters, but this has some wiggle room too—if there's a classroom or office space connected to your library, an architect could potentially remove a wall and add extra space. If you're currently expecting to have new construction soon, you could use different parameters, but sometimes having that limitation makes you more creative.

Another fun related exercise is to challenge your students to design their own dream library space. They can use paper and pencil, a program like Minecraft, physical tools like Legos, and so on. This activity can give you insight into the types of spaces your students would love to see.

Write up a Library Wish List

We often hear stories of principals discovering that they have $1,000 in the budget that they must spend within twenty-four hours, or they will lose it. Or a major grant becomes available, but it requires an itemized budget. Thus, it makes sense to create a dream library wish list that you can have on hand. When that unexpected funding appears, you'll be ready.

When Todd Burleson's parent-teacher organization (PTO) at Hubbard Woods asked him for ideas on how to spend their money, he sent them a version of his library wish list. They asked him what else he needed, so he sent them his dream wish list, and they funded all of it (T. Burleson, personal communication, March 14, 2017)! When you discover the perfect grant that can help transform your space, you'll already have a budget ready.

Create a document organized in the way you see fit. Some prefer to organize based on the learning space (computer lab, instruction area, makerspace, etc.), while others prefer to organize by type of furnishing/purchase (chairs, tables, carts, etc.). Add links to potential vendors, contact info, and current prices. Update this list regularly.

Action Steps

Visit at least one learning space (other than your school). Take notes on what you observe.

Use Pinterest or Twitter to gather some space inspiration ideas. Designate a location to gather your inspiration, whether it is a Pinterest board, a file on your desktop, or a physical folder with color printouts.

Work with your library design team to create a mood board for your library.

Spend some time brainstorming your dream library. Start creating a wish list of items you'd love to get for your space as well as changes you'd like to make.

CHAPTER 6

Many school districts are desperately cash-strapped. This chapter offers easy, affordable solutions and hacks that can make a big difference in a school library space.

Budget-Friendly Changes

Realistically, most school districts do not have huge renovation budgets. Many budget for furniture and similar needs to be replaced only every twenty years—and even when this happens, they tend to go with the status quo of the same heavy, uncomfortable furniture they previously purchased. A lack of funds doesn't mean that meaningful changes cannot happen in your space. These changes might not be made overnight, but they are quite doable for little to no cost. It will require a bit of elbow grease and effort, but the results will be well worth it.

This chapter will look at creative changes you can make that are free (or very cheap) to implement. These changes will take more time than fulfilling a shopping list, but the outcomes can truly improve your library. I'll also discuss changes that have a minimal cost associated with them, but give lots of bang for your buck. I'll share examples from changes I made to my space, as well as those in other school libraries.

Changes That Are Free to Implement

While free changes won't dramatically transform your library, they will go a long way toward creating a new mindset within your space. Often, the resources you need are already in front of you—you just have to know where to look. As I've worked with and talked to librarians at many schools, I've been amazed at how much a library can be transformed simply by getting rid of stuff—I'll share some strategies for weeding books and furniture in the following section. You might find that there are items already in your library, school, or district that you can put to good use. Make sure that you also review Chapter 7. I go into detail there about how to source donations, which is another great way to change up your space for free.

Practice Less Is More

Many school libraries, especially older ones, have gradually accumulated stuff over the years: broken or no longer functional furniture; storage rooms filled with obsolete equipment; file cabinets stuffed with handouts about LaserDisk players and award certificates from the 1990s (which I found at Stewart Middle Magnet School in 2015). It's amazing how much stuff is retained over the years, especially if your school had several librarians (or one or two who refused to throw anything away).

Getting rid of the stuff you no longer need may sound like a ridiculously simple thing to do, but it can work wonders. Remove that out-of-date equipment. Be ruthless with your file cabinet. Repair or remove broken furniture. Consider ways that you can either get rid of such items or retrofit them into something useful. Many schools have made desks out of old encyclopedias, or coffee tables out of card catalogs.

How you remove furniture will depend on your district. In Hillsborough County Public Schools, there is paperwork that has to be approved by the principal, after which the district returns it to the furniture warehouse. If the items are in good condition, consider offering them to your teachers. I was able to give my reading teachers several book display racks that I no longer needed. It was a win-win for all of us: I had more room in my library, and they had a way to organize their classroom libraries.

It can be very tempting to immediately fill that empty space with something new, but bear in mind that open space is important, too. When working on creative projects, many students like to work low to the ground, often on the floor itself. Open some floor space by eliminating excess furniture, and you'll create new workspaces for your students. You'll also improve flow throughout your space. Erikson and Markuson caution that, "the temptation is to utilize every square foot of floor area for furniture. Leaving open spaces seems like an extravagant waste of space. However, the way a library functions is very important, and you don't want users running into obstacles at every turn. You also want the library to be inviting, and *clutter and crowding are the antithesis of an inviting environment*" (emphasis mine) (2007).

As a warning, be particularly mindful of removing items that may have sentimental significance for others in your school. If there are items in your library that you no longer need (but that other individuals have strong feelings about), be sure to have a discussion with invested parties to reach a compromise.

At Hubbard Woods School, Todd Burleson inherited dozens of quilts made by students and a teacher over the years—many of those students were adults by that time. The quilts hadn't been taken down from the walls for years and were full of dust. Todd talked to the teacher who had made the quilts, and eventually they came to the compromise of washing and displaying the quilts made by current students in other areas of the school. In this way, he was able to honor the school's tradition and still change up his library space. Now, he has students create the artwork that hangs on the walls, and he rotates it throughout the year (T. Burleson, personal communication, March 14, 2017).

Weed Your Collection

It's quite likely that your physical collection could use a good, thorough weeding. There may be out-of-date books in your collection. Certainly the curriculum and student interests have changed over the years. With the addition of ebooks and databases, our physical collections can focus more on pleasure reading and popular topics for our students. If your collection hasn't been weeded in a long time, be systematic and ruthless. Download a shelf list of every item in the library and import it into Microsoft Excel or another spreadsheet program. Delete from the spreadsheet: (1) any items that are less than five years old; and (2) any items that have been checked out in the last five (or seven, or ten) years. Feel free to use your own parameters here. Weed everything that's left. When I first started at Stewart Middle Magnet School, I weeded only items that hadn't checked out since I was born in 1984—this amounted to several thousand titles! Each year, I made my criteria stricter until my collection was in sync with the reading habits of my students.

Weed your collection thoroughly, and look for ways to shift and condense your collection to open space. If you have wall shelving, you might be able to create some new book displays with your cleared space. Or have the district remove some shelving, creating space for student work areas, murals, or interactive areas such as Lego or whiteboard walls. At Stewart Middle Magnet School, I was able to weed and shift enough books to have some shelving removed from the wall, freeing space for a whiteboard and projector for our instructional space (see Figure 6.1).

Figure 6.1 By weeding the collection at Stewart Middle Magnet, wall space was opened for a whiteboard and projector for teaching.

If you have floor stacks, consider eliminating some to open floor space. Removing furniture is one of the fastest ways to create more room in a library that has "no space left." Remove the shelves, add some stools, and create a café-height workstation for your students. If you do this, just make sure that the workstations are stable without the shelves—some might be a tipping hazard.

Todd Burleson's floor stacks were bolted to the floor at Hubbard Woods School. Over the summer, he worked with maintenance staff and a sledgehammer and ripped the shelving units from the floor. They then rebuilt each unit, adding castors for mobility, and reducing the number of shelves on each unit to create breathing room (see Figure 6.2). He had to remove all the books from the shelves to do this, which led to a reevaluation of the collection and a lot of weeding (T. Burleson, personal communication, March 14, 2017).

Figure 6.2 The rebuilt mobile shelving units at Hubbard Woods School in Winnetka, Illinois. *Photo by Todd Burleson.*

Use District Resources

School districts often have furniture warehouses where discarded, but usable, furniture is stored. Find out if your district has such a space and, if it does, pay it a visit. You might be able to creatively reuse an item intended for something else, such as repurposing a broken mobile Smart Board into a mobile Lego wall. Or you might discover things that are already designed with flexibility and mobility in mind, like small cafeteria tables. Furniture from district warehouses doesn't cost you anything but time, and it can help to quickly and easily change your environment.

Be sure to look around your school for unused or neglected items. I was able to have a whiteboard moved by our district from our copy room (why did we need one there?) to our library, creating a space for teaching and presentations. If you're looking for something specific, ask your teachers, administration, and custodial staff. You might be surprised by what you find.

In addition to utilizing physical resources within your district, look into the services that your district provides. Every school and district is different, but it's possible that your custodial and/or maintenance staff can help you with some of your transformation projects. See if they can help move furniture to a new location, add castors to existing furniture, take down or hang up shelves, paint the walls a new color, and so on. It never hurts to ask.

ISTE STANDARDS CONNECTION

ISTE Standards for Educators 1. Educators continually improve their practice by learning from and with others and exploring proven and promising practices that leverage technology to improve student learning

By researching the examples of other school libraries and how they were able to transform their spaces on tight budgets, we can effectively support our students by making affordable changes to the learning environment in our spaces.

Changes That Have a Minimal Cost

Sometimes, investing a small amount of money can go a long way. Most of us don't have huge renovation budgets (but if you do, congrats!), but we do have fundraisers. And bookfair money. And parents and community members who might chip in a few bucks to a DonorsChoose or GoFundMe project (more on using these two funding sources in Chapter 7). These are some examples of easy changes you can make that have a minimal cost associated with them.

Paint the Walls

It may seem like a simple solution, but sprucing up your space with color can do wonders to boost student creativity and engagement. Out of all the changes made to the Stewart Middle Magnet School library and makerspace in 2014, painting the walls blue and green was the change most frequently mentioned by students when asked what they liked best. Spend time thinking about what colors you'd like for your environment. Too much stimulation might make students too amped. Too dull, and it might not make much of a difference. Bring in paint swatches and have your library design team vote on their favorites. Also consider how the colors will look with current furniture, future furniture purchases, and permanent fixtures.

While paint can potentially cost money, it doesn't always have to. Find out if your school district has a department for painting. If they do, they might be willing to mix up a color for you with paint they already have—you might even be able to get them to do the painting for you. Make sure to ask local hardware stores—they are often willing to donate such supplies to schools in exchange for a mention in the school newsletter. Even if you do have to purchase paint yourself, the cost is often minimal, and a moderate fundraiser can cover it. If your district allows, invite parents, students, and community members to come in and help you paint. Getting these people involved will boost community buy-in and create a sense of unity. You can also just paint columns or an accent wall to bring in a splash of color if you cannot afford to paint the whole library.

Writable Surfaces

Writable surfaces, such as whiteboard walls, whiteboard tables, mobile whiteboards, and chalkboard walls, can be fantastic for students. While porcelain whiteboard tables and fancy mobile whiteboards can be very expensive, there are a lot of great, DIY solutions that are very affordable and have great results.

Whiteboard Paint

Whiteboard paint can work on any paintable smooth surface and transform it into a writeable dry erase surface. It is more expensive than regular paint (between $100 and $250 in general, depending on the brand and the size of the wall to be covered). Since it is effective in creating interactive environments, you can often write a microgrant, ask your PTSA, or see if a local store will donate it. A DonorsChoose project funded the paint for the whiteboard wall at Stewart Middle Magnet School (see Figure 6.3 and see Chapter 7 for more on DonorsChoose.org). Don't use the cheap brands, as they wear out much faster. While there will be some ghosting of dry-erase markers and some discoloration, as long as you clean a surface painted with whiteboard paint regularly, it should last several years before you need to repaint it. To make sure that you get the best use possible out of your whiteboard paint, make sure to do the following:

- Sand the area to be painted thoroughly. You want the smoothest surface possible. Use an electric sander if one is available. Do NOT use whiteboard paint on cinder block—dry erase markers are not able to write well on a rough surface.

- Use at least one or two coats of primer first, more if the wall is not already white.

- Follow the directions on the whiteboard paint to the letter. There are often weird, complicated instructions such as how long to wait between coats, when to mix it, and so on. If you don't follow the directions, your whiteboard paint will not cure correctly.

Figure 6.3 The whiteboard wall at Stewart Middle Magnet School was created using whiteboard paint.

Shower Board

Shower board is a type of medium density fiberboard used in shower installations. It has a white, shiny surface that can be written on with a dry-erase marker. Many teachers purchase this at home supply stores and have it cut down into small, individual student whiteboards. Individual whiteboards can work well in library instruction, but there are other ways to use shower board as well. It can be mounted to a wall to create an instant whiteboard wall—this works well for walls that have uneven surfaces or when you aren't allowed to paint. You can also cut shower board to size for tables. It could be screwed, glued, or even duct taped onto your existing tables, turning them into whiteboard tables for a fraction of the cost.

Figure 6.4 The Wonder Wall at Hubbard Woods School was created using shower board. *Photo by Todd Burleson.*

At Hubbard Woods School, Todd Burleson didn't just want a whiteboard wall—he wanted a whiteboard hallway. Due to the size of the area, using whiteboard paint would have been very expensive. But he was able to source shower board at the cost of $12 for a 4' x 8' sheet. By using shower board, he was able to create a 300-square-foot wonder wall in his library for less than the cost of a new wall mounted porcelain whiteboard (see Figure 6.4). Students use this space to brainstorm ideas, ask questions, and of course, to wonder (T. Burleson, personal communication, March 14, 2017).

Be sure to clean your shower board regularly, preferably using brand-name whiteboard cleaner. If left uncleaned, dry-erase markings can become permanent. Shower boards are also prone to scratching, and you will likely need to replace them every few years.

Glass

Panes of glass can be a creative and affordable dry erase solution. Many colleges, universities, and high school libraries have purchased affordable glass tabletops from stores like IKEA and then mounted them on their walls. The wall behind the glass can be the same color as the rest of the wall, or it can be a different color or design. You can also use existing windows in your library for this same purpose.

Glass wipes off easily and looks clean and professional. However, glass can be easily broken and vandalized, so use caution in where and how you install it.

Add Mobility to Furniture

Not everyone can afford to buy brand new flip and nest tables on casters right away. However, you can retrofit many traditional types of library and classroom furniture. Hardware stores carry sets of castors for purchase (ask to see if these can be donated). It usually only takes a few minutes to install these, and you can have mobile furniture. Try to get casters that can lock if possible—having your furniture be too mobile can make the environment chaotic. Try putting casters on tables, chairs, even bookcases (see Figure 6.2). When in doubt as to whether or not it's OK or safe to add casters to an individual piece of furniture, ask your maintenance staff for advice. Also, consider other methods of sprucing up your existing furniture, such as painting it (colors or whiteboard paint), refinishing it, or changing the height. All of these changes can be quite affordable.

Examples of DIY Solutions

Librarians are natural DIY types; they make the best of the resources available to them, and find solutions. So, of course, there are plenty of amazing DIY solutions we can implement that can have a significant impact on our spaces. Often, DIY changes add more character to a space than spending a ton of money to have a designer create it.

Figure 6.5 DIY book coffee table at Shorecrest Preparatory School in St. Petersburg, Florida.

Physical Space Changes

DIY changes to your physical space can be extremely fun and easy to implement. Often, students can help with these projects, which creates more opportunity for student voice and buy-in in your space. Some changes do require purchasing supplies, but usually, the cost is minimal. Here are some changes you can make to your space on a relatively small budget.

DIY book coffee table. All it takes is a quick search on Pinterest to find instructions for a DIY book coffee table. In fact, there are TONS of projects out there that use recycled books. When you do that massive weeding to create more space in your library, save some of those books for DIY projects. Old reference books work especially well for this. At Shorecrest Preparatory School in St. Petersburg, Florida, they topped their coffee book table with a board that they created a word search on, allowing for a sense of playfulness and even more interactivity in their library (see Figure 6.5).

DIY Mobile whiteboards. The book *Make Space* is a fantastic resource from Stanford's d.school. While the book focuses on higher education, many of the projects and examples apply to K–12 schools. They include detailed instructions for creating your own affordable, mobile whiteboard using supplies you can source from hardware stores and online. They also include instructions for modular tables, foam cubes, and more (Doorley and Whitthoft, 2010).

Stand-alone shelving to café table. Many stand-alone shelving units are bulky and sturdy. If you have one that's empty after weeding, consider removing all the shelves and adding some café-height stools. You've got an instant café table that was free! If your district supports refinishing furniture, consider getting it refinished in a new color to set it apart from the remaining shelving.

Simple Non-Space Changes

Not every change has to involve changing the physical space of your library. Changes to how students and teachers use and interact with the space can also have a significant impact. Consider some of these simple additions for your library:

Student health-supply station. Many students either can't afford or forget to bring with them basic health necessities. Consider soliciting donations or using discretionary funds to purchase items that students might need. Wendy Lopez keeps items such as lotion, tissues, hand sanitizer, and cough drops available for her students at Santa Fe Catholic High School.

Student school-supply station. Likewise, many students either can't afford or forget their basic school supplies. Instead of punishing or reprimanding students for forgetting a pencil/glue stick/construction paper, create a student supply station in your library where students can get the supplies they need. Look into getting donations for this section; There are many charitable organizations and education foundations that donate school supplies.

Coffee center. This one works best for high schools. Something as simple as a Keurig coffee machine, a K-Cup dispenser that charges a minimal fee, and some styrofoam coffee cups can greatly change the culture of your library (and attract more students). While we're on the subject, consider designating a café space in the library where food and drinks are allowed. Adults love to work in coffee shops where they have snacks and drinks—why shouldn't we provide the same resources for our students?

Figure 6.6a Before: The Hubbard Woods School library hallway. *Photo by Todd Burleson.*

Figure 6.6b After: The Hubbard Woods School library Lego hallway. *Photo by Todd Burleson.*

 LIBRARY PROFILE

SCHOOL: Hubbard Woods School in Winnetka, Illinois

STAFF: Todd Burleson, librarian

GRADES: K–4

When Todd Burleson became the librarian at Hubbard Woods School in 2010, the library was a crowded mess. The shelves were so packed full of books that students couldn't pull one out without several others falling out as well. There was no clear organization system for the collection. The previous librarian had been there for thirty-five years and had never gotten rid of anything. In addition to the neglected collection, the library still housed out-of-date technology, including LaserDisk players and filmstrip projectors. Todd said that the library felt sleepy and neglected, and it was immediately noticeable when you entered the room.

The library had a lot of things going for it. The school was nearing its 100th birthday. The library is housed in the original gymnasium, making for high ceilings, lots of natural light, and plenty of exposed brick. Todd wanted to transform the library into a space that was "full of excitement, passion, and was visually inspiring for students." Todd kept one each of the old technology and got rid of the rest. He turned what he saved into a minimuseum and research project for his students (see the back wall in Figure 6.8).

One of the biggest problems in the space was that the shelving was bolted to the floor. In the summer of 2010, Todd worked with the maintenance crew to dismantle and rebuild the shelves into mobile shelving units (see Figure 6.2). He continued to tweak and adjust the space for several years. Then in 2014, the school's PTO had money to spend that they had saved up for the school's 100th anniversary. Todd gave them a wish list, and they asked him what else he wanted. Eventually, they gave him a total budget of $30,000 to transform the library into the IDEA Lab. The money was used to purchase new furniture, storage cabinets, shelving, organizational supplies, etc. That summer, the library was transformed into a vibrant STEM hub. They created a Lego wall hallway (Figure 6.6b), where students could build and tinker. They installed shower board to create a wonder wall where students could brainstorm and doodle (Figure 6.4). The computer lab transformed into a tinkering studio (Figure 6.8). The library has dynamically changed, and the teachers and students love it. (T. Burleson, personal communication, March 14, 2017)

Figure 6.7 The Hubbard Woods School library in Winnetka, Illinois. *Photo by Todd Burleson.*

Figure 6.8 One of the makerspace areas in the Hubbard Woods School library. *Photo by Todd Burleson.*

Figure 6.9 Green screen production room in the Hubbard Woods School library. *Photo by Todd Burleson.*

 Action Steps

Get rid of unnecessary furniture. Look around your library and see if there's broken or unneeded furniture. Have the district remove it.

Weed your collection. Do a thorough evaluation of your collection, and condense and shift it where needed.

Discuss low-cost DIY changes with your library design team. You might be surprised what gets them the most excited, and they might know about potential resources (such as parents or businesses) that can help.

CHAPTER 7

Most school districts do not have a budget dedicated to library renovations and improvements. This chapter focuses on ways to source funding through donations, crowdfunding, and grants.

Funding Redesign Projects

Money is one of the most common factors holding schools back from transforming their library spaces. Our budgets are often pitiful at best. Many schools struggle to fund even a modest book budget, let alone a technology or furniture budget. We can let this keep us from making the changes we know our students need, or we can stop making excuses, roll up our sleeves, and put in the hard work of finding the funding we need to transform learning in our libraries.

Sourcing Donations

We often think of donations for regular school supplies, such as paper, pencils, and tissues. Classroom supply wish lists are pretty standard in most schools. Our parent and community members want to help support our schools. Unfortunately, they don't always know what is needed. By soliciting their donations (and thanking them of course), we can empower our community members to play a vital part in reimagining our library spaces.

Supply Drives

A supply drive or wish list for specific supplies can go a long way in getting your students what they need in your library. Obviously, not all parents are going to donate $500 tables, but they are quite likely to give supplies that are affordable and easy to source.

When I started the makerspace at Stewart Middle Magnet School, I held a Lego drive. Everyone who donated a Ziploc bag of Legos was entered into a drawing for a gift card. During this drive, many parents also offered other makerspace tools that they had at home, such as arts and craft supplies, K'NEX, and tools. These donations helped us to kick-start the makerspace, and they helped our parents and students to become a part of the creation process.

At Christie Elementary School in Plano, Texas, STEM Coach Jessica Malloy found a great solution for sourcing supply donations for their learning commons. In the main hallway of the school, there is a giving tree (see Figure 7.1). It has cards for various supplies needed by the learning commons and maker-space, such as duct tape, Amazon gift cards, and Play-Doh. Parents and community members can take cards, bring in donations, and know that they are making a tangible difference in the learning experiences of their students (J. Malloy, personal communication, March 18, 2017). Read more on Christie Elementary School in the profile at the end of this chapter.

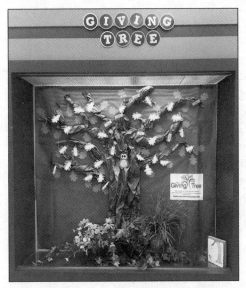

Figure 7.1 The Giving Tree at Christie Elementary School in Plano, Texas. *Photo by Jessica Malloy.*

Fundraisers and Book Fairs

Fundraisers have long been a staple of funding projects at schools. Be sure to check with the rules of your district, but librarians are usually allowed to have at least one fundraiser a year, not including bookfairs. Having a specific goal or target for your fundraiser will help to build excitement and increase the funds you're able to raise. Let your community know why you're raising (a new teaming table, an audio recording studio, charging lockers, or other renovations). Once you've raised funds and purchased the new equipment, make sure to share it with your community and thank them for their support.

Beyond regular fundraisers, bookfairs are excellent tools for transforming your space. Many book fair companies, such as Scholastic, offer furniture and technology that you can purchase with your book fair funds. You can also take cash payment and use that toward the things you need to redesign your space.

Don't be afraid to ask directly for money. At Christie Elementary School, the teachers and administration put together a compelling video about their vision for their learning commons and what they wanted to achieve (see the video at youtube.com/watch?v=AAiQt2Dz7ug). In addition, Jessica Malloy created a $30,000 to $50,000 itemized wish list detailing the kinds of furniture and changes they wanted to make. They shared the video and wish list with community members, local churches, and individuals, and eventually raised $20,000 through their campaign—all this at a Title I school! (J. Malloy, personal communication, March 18, 2017).

In-kind donations

Local businesses often love to donate to schools in exchange for a mention in the school newsletter. This can work especially well with things like paint, building supplies and tools. Also, consider soliciting offices for the technology that they no longer use. Many offices will donate computers, monitors, and other new technology in good condition for a tax write-off. Sometimes they might also have furniture and storage supplies to off-load as well. Todd Burleson received donations of binder storage towers from local offices. He ended up deciding not to use them for binders—now one tower holds K'NEX, and another organizes consumable craft supplies (T. Burleson, personal communication, March 14, 2017). Read more about Todd's story in Chapter 6.

Crowdfunding

Crowdfunding has gained popularity in recent years and is an excellent way for schools to raise funds for projects. The basic idea of crowdfunding is to present a project and wish list of items for which you are raising funds. You create a short narrative (and sometimes a video) about the project and why it is important, and you solicit donations. The fantastic thing about crowdfunding is that it allows everyone to help, no matter their finances. People can donate $5 or $500; they are playing an active part in improving education for kids. Don't limit your pool of potential donors to only parents and community members—people will often donate to schools that they have little or no connection to because they believe in the project itself. Make sure you check with your district offices, as not every district allows schools to use crowdfunding sites.

ISTE STANDARDS CONNECTION

ISTE Standards for Educators 1c. Educators stay current with research that supports improved student learning outcomes, including findings from the learning sciences.

Sourcing funds through donations, crowdsourcing, and grants takes research and reflection. Doing so allows us to use digital tools and resources in our spaces effectively and can help us to spur student innovation and creativity.

DonorsChoose

DonorsChoose.org is a fantastic source for crowdfunding education projects. It is currently available only to public schools. After you create a profile, you can create a project with an essay and a wish list, and anyone can donate any amount of money to help it succeed. It's best to focus on smaller projects at first, as they have a greater chance of being funded. To receive supplies through DonorsChoose, the entire project must be funded by the deadline. The first project you create must use DonorsChoose vendors; after that, you can use outside vendors, but there is an additional charge (in points). Organizations often have match offers for specific types of projects, such as those that are STEM related or incorporate the arts. These matches are a fantastic way to raise money quickly because you only need to raise half the funds.

At Stewart Middle Magnet School, we raised over $10,000 in funds through DonorsChoose projects over approximately four years. The projects included supplies, tools, and technology for our makerspace. A DonorsChoose project funded the epic Lego wall (see Figure 7.3), as well as the whiteboard wall (search Lego wall or whiteboard wall on RenovatedLearning.com for tutorials). We also raised funds for a set of six Hokki stools that allow students to wiggle and fidget while they work (see Figure 7.2).

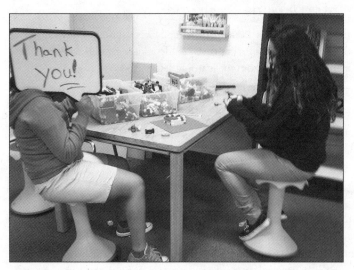

Figure 7.2 Hokki stools at Stewart Middle Magnet that were purchased through DonorsChoose.

GoFundMe

Another great crowdfunding platform is GoFundMe. GoFundMe allows anyone to create a project to raise funds. One of the great things about this platform is that you can use the money while it's being raised, so you can make changes gradually. There's an unlimited amount of time to raise funds, and you can use the site to fundraise for just about anything.

Kickstarter

Kickstarter is different and more complicated than the other two platforms here, but it is worth mentioning. In general, Kickstarter tends to focus on larger, innovative projects—this isn't a platform for funding a few tables or supplies. Kickstarter can be useful for large, innovative redesign projects. It can also be an excellent platform for raising funds for a library rebuild after a natural disaster, such as a tornado or flood.

One amazing Kickstarter success story comes from the students at REALM Charter School in Berkley, California. The school had no library at all, so students in the school's Studio H Design and Build class decided to design one themselves. They brainstormed what they wanted their library to look like, and they eventually developed a prototype for a shelving/storage unit that was modular and flexible. The books didn't sit in neat rows, encouraging students to browse and serendipitously find books to read. The students created a video and posted their project on Kickstarter. In one month, they raised $79,000 to build their shelves and stock their library with books (Zaslow, 2014)! While not every school will be able to raise this kind of money on Kickstarter, it's an option to keep in mind for big dream projects.

Grants

When it comes to funding larger projects, and projects tied to academic goals, grants are an excellent way to go. Grants often involve more work than crowdfunding or soliciting donations, but the payoff can be big. The size of grants vary widely: $100 to $500 grants are common with smaller, local organizations; $1,000 to $5,000 grants are often available for schools; and. if you're working on a massive project, federal grants can be even higher. Whatever type of project or transformation you're looking into for your library space, there's likely a grant for it.

Figure 7.3 The Lego wall at Stewart Middle Magnet School was funded for under $500 through DonorsChoose.

Microgrants

Microgrants are often given by smaller, local organizations and have less competition than higher dollar grants. They typically run between $100 and $500. That might not sound like much, but with some planning and ingenuity, a grant of that size can add a lot to your library.

To find microgrants, subscribe to the email newsletters of local associations and organizations. Specific places to consider are your teachers' union, local education foundations, and your state library association.

Here are some examples of library projects that you could fund with grants of this size:

- Labels and signage materials to "generify" your library collection, making it easier for students to find the books they need, and increasing circulation.

- A rug, bean bag chairs, and small table to create a cozy reading nook to encourage reading for pleasure.

- A coffee maker, supplies, and café tables to create a mini-café for students, increasing alertness and providing a comfortable atmosphere for study.

- Whiteboard paint and dry erase markers to create an interactive library space (approximately $300).

- Lego baseplates and supplies to build a Lego wall (approximately $500) (see Figure 7.3). Visit my blog post for a detailed supply list and instructions: www.renovatedlearning.com/2014/09/12/ the-epic-library-lego-wall-how-to-build-one/.

Mid-Sized Grants

Mid-sized grants tend to run between $1,000 and $5,000, although there are some that fall outside this range. These grants have more competition than microgrants, but that shouldn't deter you from applying. Even if you don't get the first ones for which you apply, you'll be learning valuable skills and building your grant-writing toolbox, making it easier to work on future grants.

Grants at this level come from a variety of sources, but most of them tend to be companies or foundations. Some organizations are more education focused than others. Some groups are broad in their focus. To find grants related to schools and school libraries, be sure to sign up for email lists with grant opportunities, such as Mackin Grant Channel, GetEdFunding, and Demco Grants Search.

Here are some examples of projects you could fund with a mid-sized grant:

- Replacing library furniture in one particular area, such as the instructional space, with flexible, collaborative furniture that is better able to adapt to the learning needs of students.

- A teaming table to support collaborative student device use.

- A Mac desktop with GarageBand and music recording equipment to create a student podcasting/recording space.

- Paint for a green screen wall, two iPads, and software for creating a student-produced morning show/video production space.

- A set of Chromebooks, tablets, or other small devices for student use in the library.

- Several comfortable, modular couches to create a comfortable reading and study area for students.

Federal Grants

Federal grants are *much* larger than micro- and mid-level grants. For a grant of this size, you will likely be working with your school district's grants office. These types of grants are for projects far beyond adding new books to the collection or buying a few comfy chairs. We're talking about building a brand new library, taking on a massive renovation project, or replacing a library collection after a natural disaster, such as a flood or fire. Since the scope of this book focuses more on the work of individual librarians and schools in transforming their spaces, we won't address federal grant writing. For more information, search "federal grant writing" on Amazon.com to see a list of countless books written on the subject.

Tips for Finding and Writing Grants

Over the six years that it took to transform the library at Stewart Middle Magnet School, I was able to secure over $15,000 in grants and other funding for our space. I wrote many grants during this time, and I learned a lot in the process. Following are some of my best tips (adapted from renovatedlearning. com/2014/10/13/10-tips-for-writing-grant-proposals/) for finding and writing grants that get funded.

Become a Grant Reader

One of the best ways to learn how to write grants that get funded is to spend time reading a variety of other people's grant applications. Find an organization that's looking for grant reader volunteers, and sign up. Being a grant reader gives you a feel for how the grant writing process works. This behind-the-scenes look offers you valuable insight into what types of things grantors want to see. It will help you to learn firsthand what mistakes can kill a proposal, and what details can make one stand out.

Research and Design

Research everything about the organization from which you're seeking a grant. Most organizations provide a great deal of useful information on their website. Look for things such as a mission and vision statement, FAQs, examples of previously funded projects, and so on. Search for rules or stipulations about the grants. Print out what you find, read it over, and highlight important keywords and phrases.

After researching, design and tailor your grant project to the organization's vision. Look for ways to incorporate those keywords and phrases. In 2014, I knew that we needed to get flexible, collaborative furniture for our library. Lowes Toolbox for Education was looking to provide permanent physical improvements to schools that would boost community involvement, so I focused my grant proposal on how our community uses our library space (family nights, PTSA activities, bookfairs, Great American Teach-In), and I highlighted how this new furniture would help to facilitate that community involvement. And we got the grant!

Follow All Grant Instructions to the Letter

Nothing kills a grant proposal faster than ignoring the grantor's rules and parameters. If they want your essay to be no more than 500 words, a 650-word essay won't work. If they request an itemized budget, be as detailed as possible. When I volunteered as a grant reader, I saw numerous grants disqualified because they simply didn't follow the ground rules set by the grantor.

Show Your Work and Focus on Students

Grantors want to know that the money they're giving you will be used well. Show what you're already doing in your library that fits with your goal. If you have a bin of Legos in the corner that students tinker with, share its impact. If you have a reading nook that's well loved and used by students but needs an upgrade, share how many students use it, and how many books are checked out.

In addition to showing what you're already doing, make sure that you keep the focus of your grant on your students. Share their stories. Talk about how they rise above the odds. Even if the grant you're writing is for something for which you will be the primary user (e.g., a tablet for teaching classes), keep the focus on how it will impact your students, rather than how it will make your life easier.

Don't Complain

Your district's funding might be horrible. Your administration might not be supportive. You might be struggling with a less than ideal space. Whatever you do, don't spend precious page space complaining about what you don't have. Negativity turns off grant readers because it makes you sound desperate. Focus instead on the positive—the resiliency of your students, how you've made the best of a not-so-great situation. A hopeful outlook is more likely to generate excitement for your proposed project.

Proofread!

We expect our students to correct their papers, so why do we not proofread our grants? Go over it several times to make sure that there's no spelling or grammatical errors, parts that don't make sense, and so on. Always spell out acronyms and explain concepts and pedagogy. Ask someone outside of education to read it as well—they might be able to point out jargon and other things that won't be clear if your grant reader isn't an educator.

Follow Up

If you get a grant, awesome! Make sure to follow up with the organization, send a thank you card and ask about next steps. If you didn't get it, that's OK. Communicate with the organization, and ask for feedback. Sometimes they will offer tips and advice that will improve your grant-writing skills and help you secure funding next time.

 LIBRARY PROFILE

> **SCHOOL:** Christie Elementary School in Plano, Texas
> **STAFF:** Jessica Malloy, STEM coach
> **GRADES:** PK–5

The library at Christie Elementary School in Plano, Texas, was the largest room in the school, which is Title I and serves over 700 students. The collection was well maintained, and classes came to the library on a fixed schedule for book checkout and library lessons. But the principal of the school wanted it to be something more. Jessica Malloy, the STEM coach, began working with the principal, assistant principal, and librarian to plan the library's transformation into a learning commons.

Inspired by other learning commons spaces and librarians she had spoken to on Twitter, Jessica wanted to create a space that was a hybrid model: part science museum, part literacy and learning center. Keeping the books a part of the library was imperative to the school—they didn't want the transformation to take away from reading. Rather, the goal was to create new experiences for their students, to embrace literacy, provide student ownership, and create a flexible learning environment.

Figure 7.4a **Before::** The Christie Learning Commons at Christie Elementary School in Plano, Texas. *Photo by Jessica Malloy.*

Figure 7.4b **After**: The Christie Learning Commons at Christie Elementary School in Plano, Texas. *Photo by Jessica Malloy.*

Jessica put together an itemized wish list, ranging from $30,000 to $50,000 for the types of furnishings and changes they wanted to make in the space. Before making any changes, the teachers of the school put together a video with their vision for what the learning commons could be. The school then partnered with the PTA and showed this video to potential donors. By organizing and campaigning with their community, the school was able to raise $20,000 through community and individual donations!

The first step was to go through all the books and get rid of shelving to open floor space. This took an entire summer. After that, the district painted the library in bright colors geared toward promoting a creative atmosphere. Jessica met with a focus group of students who were asked to brainstorm ideas for the library. Anything they could imagine was on the table—one kindergartner even suggested a swimming pool.

That fall, they began to outfit the space. The campus technology assistant helped to build benches and tables for the makerspace. Teachers gathered recycled materials to create an alphabet wall (see Figure 7.5). They installed a giant Lego wall. They created decorations on other walls that encouraged student creativity, such as a giant light-up "C" with the four Cs of creativity, collaboration, communication and critical thinking (see Figure 7.6) and an explore clock display (see Figure 7.7). By creatively sourcing materials to create a sense of wonder and explora-tion, Jessica was able to transform the space completely. She emphasizes that, "what we do in our space has to enhance the curriculum. Teachers can apply what they learn in the classroom in a whole new way." The space is now unlike anything else in the school building (J. Malloy, personal communication, March 18, 2017).

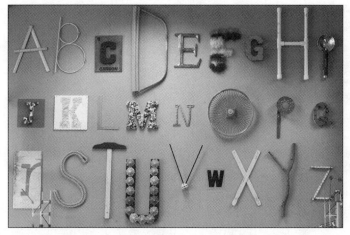

Figure 7.5 The teacher-created alphabet wall at Christie Elementary School in Plano, Texas. *Photo by Jessica Malloy.*

Figure 7.6 The Four Cs decorate the wall at the Christie Learning Commons. *Photo by Jessica Malloy.*

Figure 7.7 Even the clock in the Christie Learning Commons encourages students to explore. *Photo by Jessica Malloy.*

 Action Steps

Prioritize what needs funding. Review the dream library wish list you created in Chapter 5. Are there items on that list that can be sourced through donations or crowdfunding? Start working on those first.

Look into a grant. Spend some time browsing educational grants resource sites. Find a grant that fits one of your goals and fill out the grant application.

CHAPTER 8

While lots of improvements can be made in a library space quickly, it is wise to plan for the future. I'll discuss how to create a long-term plan for your library space, how to handle larger renovation projects, and strategies for working with architects while building a new library.

Planning for the Long Term

So far, we've focused primarily on changes and transformations in your space that take place over a short time period, but it behooves us to be prepared with a plan for the future. An unexpected opportunity to make a significant change in our library may present itself, and we need to prepare for it. Having a plan in place also helps us to be methodical and intentional about the changes we make. Rather than constantly experimenting with new furniture, technology, and room arrangements, we can make changes that work toward a larger goal.

In this chapter, I'll also address two of the fantastic opportunities that sometimes come our way: large renovation projects that revamp an existing library and the construction of a new library building. I'll also take some time to reflect on the future of school libraries and what they might look like in the years to come.

Creating a Five-Year Plan for Your Library

To be intentional about transforming your space beyond the immediate future, you should create a five-year plan for your library. Obviously, we can't predicate everything that will happen in the next five years. Technology and our students are changing radically each year, and we can't anticipate every one of our needs. That doesn't mean we shouldn't have a clear idea of our direction and our goals for our space. By creating a five-year plan and thinking through things like big ideas, district and school initiatives, technology, and funding, we can be more prepared for what might come our way.

Your plan should detail where you expect your library program to go, and what you need to make that happen. School library construction and media specialists Erikson and Markuson recommend including a vision statement, mission statement, needs assessment (our earlier survey fills this role), program goals and measurable objectives, program activities, and a projection of future needs and growth. You should also consider how these tie in with national and state standards (2007).

A five-year plan is also extremely useful if you get the opportunity to work on new construction or a renovation (more on these in the following section). Erikson and Markuson remind us that, "having a plan that articulates your program, its human activities, and attendant space requirements will help the architect understand the overall picture" (2007, p. 10).

Planning for Your Really Big Ideas

If you've followed the action steps throughout the book, at this point you've surveyed your community, formed a focus group, read up on learning space design theory, and sourced plenty of great ideas and inspiration for your space. You've probably already begun to make small changes that are having a significant impact in your library. Without doubt, some of the ideas you've come up with are big, *really* big. Maybe you want to replace ALL the furniture in your library, or tear down a few walls to create space. Maybe you have a dream to transform the copy room into an amazing makerspace or technology lab. These are all fantastic ideas, but they aren't things that will just happen overnight.

Your five-year plan is the place to create goals for your really big ideas. Projects like these often aren't doable in one school year, unless you're lucky enough to have a large renovation budget or substantial grant. Break down your really big idea into achievable goals. Here is an example of one of these big ideas and how you might break it down in your five-year plan:

 ## TUTORIAL

Really Big Idea: Replacing ALL the Furniture in the Library

- Pick one area of your library (such as the instructional large group space), and focus on that area first.

- Discuss your vision for your space with your administration.

- Spend some time reviewing vendor catalogs for ideas. Visit education conferences to see furniture in person. Talk to vendors and get samples to show to your community.

- Create a plan for how much furniture you will need for this space, and include a tentative budget.

- Look for ways that you could break the budget into phases (e.g., chairs one year, tables the next). Find out if it's possible to get funds from your district.

- Research and write grants. Consider crowdfunding and other sources.

- As funds become available, begin purchasing and adding new furniture to the space. Hint: Once you have a finalized budget, talk with your vendor about pricing. Many vendors will offer bulk discounts to work with your budget.

- Repeat with other sections of the library until all furniture is replaced.

Planning for Future District Initiatives

More than likely, your school and/or district have a five-year plan for future initiatives. Locate this plan, study it, and look for how the school library fits in with and supports this plan. Is your district planning to start supporting BYOD? Is there a 1:1 initiative coming? Find out as much as you can. If your district and/or school have a committee that focuses on future planning, consider joining. It will be a lot of work, but it's good to have a voice for libraries on such a committee, and it can help you to advocate for the importance of your role and space.

It's also a good idea to sit down with your principal and discuss his/her vision of your school's future, and what role the library will play in that vision. Things like a greater push toward student independent learning, collaborative project-based learning, and teacher professional development plans will influence what you put into your five-year plan. For example, if the push is toward creating an environment of student independence and leadership, you could incorporate creating a self-checkout system into your five-year plan like the one Andy Plemmons has at Barrow Elementary (see Figure 8.1. More on Barrow at the end of this chapter). And, as we discussed in Chapter 4, incorporating your school's mission and vision into your library is a vital way to remain relevant as the hub of your school.

Figure 8.1 The custom built self-checkout station at Barrow Elementary School library in Athens, Georgia. *Photo by Andy Plemmons.*

Planning for Future Technology Needs

Technology is changing at an incredibly fast pace, so it can be difficult to plan too far ahead in this realm. There is no doubt that it will continue to play a huge role in education, so as we make our five-year plan, we must take it into account. In Chapter 3, I touched on many different ways that technology is used and supported in the school library. Revisit your notes on that chapter and use them to aid in planning how technology will play a role in your five-year plan.

Here are some questions to ask during this phase:

- What types of devices is the district planning to support and emphasize? Are they considering BYOD or 1:1?

- How will you make device charging and power available to students and teachers?

- Will the library be checking out devices to students?

- How many desktops will you need? Do you want to have desktops?

- What types of specialized technology do you want to add (e.g., video editing software, green screen, 3-D printer, etc.)?

- Will there be a district computer refresh?

Planning for Funding

Funding a redesign project isn't always easy, but as we saw in Chapter 7, it is possible. As you write your five-year plan, make sure to take into account how you will fund your transformation. District funds, grants, crowdfunding, and donations will all likely play a role in your plan. If you're not sure at this point exactly how everything will be funded, that's OK. Make a list of potential funding sources for each of your ideas and then move from there.

As you design your plan, research the changes you want to make and create an estimated budget. Research vendors and compare prices. Look for ways that you can break up larger projects into smaller, more affordable chunks. Arm yourself with as much information as possible. Then, if you're lucky enough to be told about an extra $1,000 that your principal has to spend tomorrow, you'll be ready with a budget in hand.

Most grants require you to have a detailed budget for what you plan to purchase. By planning funding and creating a budget for your really big ideas now, you will be more prepared when you discover a grant opportunity that fits with your idea. If you need help thinking of different ideas and budget ranges for projects, check out Appendix A. It organizes the different projects mentioned in this book by budget range.

Renovation and New Construction

Renovations and new construction projects are both unique opportunities to create and transform a library space. While not exactly the same, these opportunities share commonalities, such as advocating for your role in planning and working with architects. Thus, they are combined in this section.

If your school is on the older side, you might get the opportunity to work on a larger, district-funded renovation project in your library. In a renovation project, anything is on the table, from removing walls (as long as they aren't load bearing) to changing up flooring, adding windows, creating new spaces, and so on.

Advice specific to working on renovation projects appears at the end of this section.

It won't happen in every librarian's career, but if you're lucky enough, you might get the opportunity to be part of building a new library. You might open a brand new school. Or you might participate in designing a new library building to replace an existing one. New construction is an exciting, unique chance to shape a school library space from the ground up. Once you know that such a project is happening, it's vital to plan and advocate for your role right away.

Advocating for Your Role in Planning

Unfortunately, librarians are often not included in the planning process of both renovations and construction projects. Advocate early for your role in the planning and creation of your new space. Dr. Ross Todd reminds us that "school librarians clearly bring expertise to [the library design] process: they know how students learn through information, individually, in groups, and in classes, how this learning is best maximized through infrastructure, organization management and spatial arrangement of information resources" (Erikson and Markson, 2007). You have a unique understanding of school library spaces and the needs of students, teachers, and guests in those spaces. If you stand by and do not advocate for your role, it is possible that you will be left out of the design process. This could mean that you aren't a part of important conversations, such as what level of print materials and technology the new space will have, how much workspace is needed, staffing requirements, and so on. Without the voice of the librarian, your school could end up with a beautiful new library that doesn't function smoothly. Make sure to join any committees working on planning, working with the architect, and so on.

ISTE STANDARDS CONNECTION

ISTE Standards for Educators 2: Educators seek out opportunities for leadership to support student empowerment and success and to improve teaching and learning.

We must plan ahead for our spaces, exercise leadership, and be advocates for our libraries and students. We must be a part of the decision-making process to have an impact on the learning of our students.

Working with Architects and Vendors

Working with architects and vendors on a renovation or construction process can be challenging, rewarding, frustrating, and just about everything in between. Good architects will be excited to work with the school, open to exploring new concepts of library spaces, and willing to listen to your input. Not-so-good architects might be married to very traditional notions of school libraries. Or, they might want to create a library that has stunning architecture but isn't very functional or practical. If at all possible, try to be a part of selecting the architect. A good architect who's open and willing to listen will make the process much easier and more rewarding. If you do end up with an architect that isn't your first choice, make sure to advocate for your role and your space. But remember, ultimately, this is their profession, and they want to do a good job.

If you went through the action steps in Chapter 4, you are already armed with invaluable survey and focus group data, as well as careful observations about your library space. This information is valuable to architects and vendors who will be working on this project. Arrange to meet with your architect and share the data that you have collected. Share your ideas and concerns about the new space.

Ask if your architect has experiences designing schools and libraries. If possible, visit some of these spaces. If the architect doesn't have experience with school libraries, you might want to consider hiring a library design consultant. It will add to your costs, but it could save you money and frustration in the long run, as you'll likely have to live with the construction for at least thirty years (Baule, 2007).

Vendors are often involved later in the design process for new construction, though they may be involved earlier for renovation projects. Library furniture vendors may have design consultants on staff, and this can be a great help. Share the information you have gathered through your survey and focus group with your vendors—they will be able to help you to find furniture to realize your vision and will know how to find what will work for your budget.

Advice for Renovation Projects

A renovation project is unique because you already have experience in the current library. You know its ups and downs. You know the students. A renovation is limited by the current physical constraints and layouts of the existing space. But these limitations can make the design process more exciting as you figure out how to work with what you have.

The L!brary Book contains beautiful, inspiring examples of schools that went through renovation projects. If you're going through a renovation, make sure to check it out. The book is very detailed about what went into the projects, the processes used by the architects and designers, and so on. Each of the projects includes color photos and the floor plan for the library. The before-and-after pictures are stunning. There's also an entire chapter on how the designers collaborated with the students at each school to create the artwork that decorates each library.

This section includes exercises and ideas that you can use with your students. The design guidelines toward the end of the book provide another fantastic resource when working with architects and designers, as they frame the different areas and functions of libraries.

To learn more about a library space that went through a renovation project, check out the library profile of the Santa Fe Catholic High School Learning Commons in Chapter 2. They were able to take a small library and break it into several very functional zones that now serve the school.

Construction and renovation projects are both complex and detailed, but it isn't within the scope of this book to go into the specific details of these projects. For more advice and detail, consult the recommended resources below.

RECOMMENDED RESOURCES FOR CONSTRUCTION AND RENOVATION

Designing a School Library Media Center of the Future, by Rolf Erikson and Carolyn Markuson. American Library Association, 2007.

The L!brary Book, by Anooradha Iyer Siddiqi. Princeton Architectural Press, 2010.

The Language of School Design, by Prakash Nair and Randall Fielding. Designshare, 2009. Note: This book focuses on the entire school, not just the library, but contains vocabulary and advice for working with architects.

LIBRARY PROFILE

SCHOOL: Barrow Elementary School in Athens, Georgia

STAFF: Andy Plemmons, library media specialist

GRADES: PK–5

The original Barrow Elementary School was built in 1923. Like many schools, it grew in a piecemeal fashion as its population grew. The library at this time was a small space (see Figures 8.2a and 8.2b). The fixed shelving separated different areas of the library (instruction, computers, etc.), but it also limited how many students could fit in each zone. The wooden tables and non-stacking wooden chairs had to be moved by adults, as they were too heavy for students. Anytime there was a special event, such as a bookfair or author visit, the tables had to be moved against the bookshelves, which prevented student checkouts.

Figure 8.2a Before: Barrow Elementary School Library in Athens, Georgia. *Photo courtesy of Andy Plemmons.*

Figure 8.2b Before: Barrow Elementary School Library in Athens, Georgia. *Photo by Andy Plemmons.*

Thanks to an E-SPLOST (special local option sales tax), the district demolished the majority of the school and built a new school building in 2013. The district and school formed a committee to plan the new school. Andy Plemmons, library media specialist at Barrow, joined the committee and was a voice and advocate for the library. The conversation focused on what a digital age library and classroom looked like. Would the library have books? Shelves? Andy didn't want to lose the vibrant programs and activities they had already implemented. He advocated for the importance of the role of libraries in schools and shared the work that he was doing with the committee.

In 2013, the new library opened along with the new school. The vibrant, bright space was designed with students in mind. The mobile, curved shelving creates lots of reading and study nooks for students, and it is easy to rearrange and reconfigure (see Figure 8.3). This shelving allows Andy to maintain checkout during special events, such as bookfairs (see Figures 8.4 and 8.5). He can even fit an entire grade level into the space for author visits! The school is 1:1 for Grades 3–5 and has grade-level iPad carts for PK–2, so the new library doesn't have a computer lab. There are a handful of desktop computers available for students to use for projects.

Figure 8.3 Reading nook in the Barrow Elementary School Library in Athens, Georgia. *Photo by Andy Plemmons.*

Figure 8.4 The bookfair and circulation areas are able to coexist at Barrow Elementary. *Photo by Andy Plemmons.*

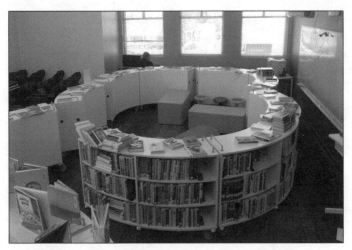

Figure 8.5 The library shelving rearranged during a bookfair at Barrow Elementary. *Photo by Andy Plemmons.*

Andy is the only staff member in the library, so he worked with the architect and designers for a plan to create a student self-checkout station (see Figure 8.1). This custom-built station allows students to return their books and place them on a shelving cart, as well as check out their books. This station frees up Andy to work with classes. Collaboration and global connections are essential parts of the library program at Barrow, so they have spaces set up for classes, small groups, video conferences, and a makerspace. They also partner with the University of Georgia, welcoming UGA students into their makerspace to work with Barrow students. To learn more about Andy's work at Barrow, visit his blog, Expect the Miraculous, at www.expectmiraculous.com.

Looking Toward the Future

We live in a dynamic and changing time for school libraries. Technology is advancing at a breakneck pace. Funding is being cut left and right. Many are questioning the roles of physical books, library spaces, and librarians. It is vital, now more than ever before, that we transform our spaces to create positive learning experiences for our students. We must continue to advocate for our role, for literacy, and for students' voices. Remember, a "thought-provoking library environment is a threshold. Its impact can inspire a lifelong habit of approaching the world with a curious intellect" (Siddiqi, 2010, p. 158). Now, more than ever, we need to create and cultivate these spaces for our students.

Libraries of the future will likely continue to shift and evolve. We are no longer the keepers of books in quiet, dust-filled rooms. Our students are learning in active, dynamic ways, and our spaces must support this, or we risk falling into irrelevancy.

It is difficult work, but it is well worth it. The future of our students is in our hands, and we have the power to make it brighter and better by reimagining our library spaces and transforming their learning experiences.

 ## Action Steps

Make a list of your really big ideas. If you have too many, focus on two or three to start. Break down your really big ideas into actionable steps. Keep the list posted where you see it every day, and begin taking action.

Start working on a five-year plan for your library. Consider your really big ideas, potential budgets, and funding sources.

Join planned or ongoing renovations at your school. If your library is part of a renovation or construction process, advocate for your role in the process as early as possible.

References

Basye, D. E., Grant, P., Hausman, S., & Johnston, T. (2015). *Get active: Reimagining learning spaces for student success.* Eugene, OR: International Society for Technology in Education.

Baule, S.M. (2007). *Facilities planning for school library and technology centers,* Second Edition. Columbus, OH: Linworth Publishing.

Bill, D. (2013, August 06). 8 Tips and Tricks to Redesign Your Classroom. Retrieved from www.edutopia.org/blog/8-tips-and-tricks-redesign-your-classroom

Cannon Design, VS Furniture, & Bruce Mau Design. (2010). *The third teacher: 79 ways you can use design to transform teaching & learning.* New York, NY: Abrams.

Diggs, V. (2015). Valerie Diggs: learning commons pioneer. *Teacher Librarian, 43*(2), 48+.

Doorley, S., & Witthoft, S. (2010). *Make space: How to set the stage for creative collaboration.* New York, NY: Abrams.

Erickson, R., & Markuson, C. (2007). *Designing a school library media center for the future.* Chicago: American Library Association.

Kelley, T., & Kelley, D. (2015). *Creative confidence: Unleashing the creative potential within us all.* London: William Collins.

Kompar, F. (2015). Re-Imagining the school library: The learning commons and systemic reform. *Teacher Librarian, 42*(4), 20+.

Loertscher, D. V., Koechlin, C., & Zwaan, S. (2008). The time is now: transform your school library into a learning commons. *Teacher Librarian, 36*(1), 8+.

Nair, P., & Fielding, R. (2005). *The language of school design: Design patterns for 21st century schools.* Minneapolis, MN: DesignShare.

Rendina, D. (2016). Six Active Learning Spaces Your Library Should Have. *AASL Knowledge Quest.* Retrieved from http://knowledgequest.aasl.org/6-active-learning-spaces-library/

Rendina, D. (2016, August 27). How to Create a Floorplan of Your Space in Excel. Retrieved from http://renovatedlearning.com/2016/08/29/floorplan-space-excel/

Rendina, D. (2016, April 18). How To Get Library Design Inspiration: 6 Places to Visit. *Renovated Learning.* Retrieved from http://renovatedlearning.com/2016/04/25/library-design-inspiration/

Siddiqi, A. I. (2010). *The l!brary book: Design collaborations in the public schools.* New York, NY: Princeton Architectural Press.

Solochek, J. S. (2014, January 10). Pasco schools aim for more modern media centers. *Tampa Bay Times.* Retrieved from www.tampabay.com/news/education/k12/pasco-schools-aim-for-more-modern-media-centers/2160573

Spencer, J., & Juliani, A. J. (2016). *LAUNCH: Using design thinking to boost creativity and bring out the maker in every student.* San Diego, CA: Dave Burgess Consulting, Inc.

Sullivan, M. L. (2013) *Library spaces for 21st century learners: A planning guide for creating new school library concepts.* Chicago, IL: American Association of School Librarians.

Thornburg, D. (2014). *From the campfire to the holodeck: Creating engaging and powerful 21st century learning environments.* San Francisco, CA: Jossey-Bass.

Recommended Resources

Groves, K., & Knight, W. (2013). *I wish I worked there!: A look inside the most creative spaces in business.* Hoboken, NJ: John Wiley & Sons Ltd.

Loertscher, D. V., Koechlin, C., & Rosenfeld, E. (2012). *The virtual learning commons: Building a participatory school learning community.* Salt Lake City, UT: Learning Commons Press.

Loertscher, D. V., Koechlin, C., & Zwaan, S. (2011). *The new learning commons: Where learners win!* Salt Lake City, UT: Learning Commons Press.

Miller, R., Casey, M., & Konchar, M. (2014). *Change your space, change your culture: How engaging workspaces lead to transformation and growth.* Hoboken, NJ: Wiley.

Salant, P., & Dillman, D. A. (1995). *How to conduct your own survey.* New York: Wiley.

Simon, N. (2011). *The participatory museum.* Santa Cruz, CA: Museum 2.0.

Sykes, J. A. (2016). *The whole school library learning commons: An educator's guide.* Santa Barbara, CA: Libraries Unlimited.

Index of Renovation Ideas by Budget

This appendix organizes ideas and projects mentioned in this book by approximate budget range. Use it as a guideline or as a source for ideas when planning your transformation.

$0-$100 Budget

$100-$500 Budget

Add Hokki stools, yoga balls, or other flexible chairs *ch 7 p.126*

Redesign library signage *ch 7 p.129*

Purchase bean bag chairs to create reading nook *ch 7 p.129*

Add café-height table and chairs (price will vary with vendor) *ch 2 p.104*

Create a DIY charging station *ch 3 p.56*

$500-1000 Budget

Paint a green screen wall and purchase iPad or other technology for video creation *ch7 p.130*

Add a charging station or charging lockers (some will be less, some more) *ch 3 p.56*

More than $1000 Budget

Create a teaming table *ch 3 p.57*

Replace furniture in one or more zones of library *ch 7 p.130*

Create a TEAL lab *ch 3 p.49*

Replace shelving *ch 7 p.105*

Create a mobile lab *ch 3, p.46*

Set up a an audio recording studio (computer, software, microphone) *ch 3 p.52*

Set up a video editing studio (iMac computer and iMovie or Final Cut) *ch 3 p.53*

Set up a photo editing or graphic design studio (computer with Photoshop, Illustrator, etc.) *ch 3 p.53*

Add whiteboard top tables *ch 2 p.29*

Add diner booths for small group zones *ch 2 p.29*

Add structural glass walls to create different learning spaces *ch 2 p.41*

Redesign your computer lab into a collaborative lab (varies) *ch 3 p.47*

ISTE Standards

ISTE Standards for Students

The ISTE Standards for Students emphasize the skills and qualities we want for students, enabling them to engage and thrive in a connected, digital world. The standards are designed for use by educators across the curriculum, with every age student, with a goal of cultivating these skills throughout a student's academic career.

1. **Empowered Learner**

   Students leverage technology to take an active role in choosing, achieving and demonstrating competency in their learning goals, informed by the learning sciences. Students:

   a. articulate and set personal learning goals, develop strategies leveraging technology to achieve them and reflect on the learning process itself to improve learning outcomes.

   b. build networks and customize their learning environments in ways that support the learning process.

   c. use technology to seek feedback that informs and improves their practice and to demonstrate their learning in a variety of ways.

   d. understand the fundamental concepts of technology operations, demonstrate the ability to choose, use and troubleshoot current technologies and are able to transfer their knowledge to explore emerging technologies.

2. Digital Citizen

Students recognize the rights, responsibilities and opportunities of living, learning and working in an interconnected digital world, and they act and model in ways that are safe, legal and ethical. Students:

a. cultivate and manage their digital identity and reputation and are aware of the permanence of their actions in the digital world.

b. engage in positive, safe, legal and ethical behavior when using technology, including social interactions online or when using networked devices.

c. demonstrate an understanding of and respect for the rights and obligations of using and sharing intellectual property.

d. manage their personal data to maintain digital privacy and security and are aware of data-collection technology used to track their navigation online.

3. Knowledge Constructor

Students critically curate a variety of resources using digital tools to construct knowledge, produce creative artifacts and make meaningful learning experiences for themselves and others. Students:

a. plan and employ effective research strategies to locate information and other resources for their intellectual or creative pursuits.

b. evaluate the accuracy, perspective, credibility and relevance of information, media, data or other resources.

c. curate information from digital resources using a variety of tools and methods to create collections of artifacts that demonstrate meaningful connections or conclusions.

d. build knowledge by actively exploring real-world issues and problems, developing ideas and theories and pursuing answers and solutions.

4. Innovative Designer

Students use a variety of technologies within a design process to identify and solve problems by creating new, useful or imaginative solutions. Students:

a. know and use a deliberate design process for generating ideas, testing theories, creating innovative artifacts or solving authentic problems.

b. select and use digital tools to plan and manage a design process that considers design constraints and calculated risks.

c. develop, test and refine prototypes as part of a cyclical design process.

d. exhibit a tolerance for ambiguity, perseverance and the capacity to work with open-ended problems.

5. Computational Thinker

Students develop and employ strategies for understanding and solving problems in ways that leverage the power of technological methods to develop and test solutions. Students:

a. formulate problem definitions suited for technology-assisted methods such as data analysis, abstract models and algorithmic thinking in exploring and finding solutions.

b. collect data or identify relevant data sets, use digital tools to analyze them, and represent data in various ways to facilitate problem-solving and decision-making.

c. break problems into component parts, extract key information, and develop descriptive models to understand complex systems or facilitate problem-solving.

d. understand how automation works and use algorithmic thinking to develop a sequence of steps to create and test automated solutions.

6. Creative Communicator

Students communicate clearly and express themselves creatively for a variety of purposes using the platforms, tools, styles, formats and digital media appropriate to their goals. Students:

    a. choose the appropriate platforms and tools for meeting the desired objectives of their creation or communication.

    b. create original works or responsibly repurpose or remix digital resources into new creations.

    c. communicate complex ideas clearly and effectively by creating or using a variety of digital objects such as visualizations, models or simulations.

    d. publish or present content that customizes the message and medium for their intended audiences.

7. Global Collaborator

Students use digital tools to broaden their perspectives and enrich their learning by collaborating with others and working effectively in teams locally and globally. Students:

    a. use digital tools to connect with learners from a variety of backgrounds and cultures, engaging with them in ways that broaden mutual understanding and learning.

    b. use collaborative technologies to work with others, including peers, experts or community members, to examine issues and problems from multiple viewpoints.

    c. contribute constructively to project teams, assuming various roles and responsibilities to work effectively toward a common goal.

    d. explore local and global issues and use collaborative technologies to work with others to investigate solutions.

© 2016 International Society for Technology in Education.

ISTE Standards for Educators

The ISTE Standards for Educators are your road map to helping students become empowered learners. These standards will deepen your practice, promote collaboration with peers, challenge you to rethink traditional approaches and prepare students to drive their own learning.

Empowered Professional

1. Learner

Educators continually improve their practice by learning from and with others and exploring proven and promising practices that leverage technology to improve student learning. Educators:

a. Set professional learning goals to explore and apply pedagogical approaches made possible by technology and reflect on their effectiveness.

b. Pursue professional interests by creating and actively participating in local and global learning networks.

c. Stay current with research that supports improved student learning outcomes, including findings from the learning sciences.

2. Leader

Educators seek out opportunities for leadership to support student empowerment and success and to improve teaching and learning. Educators:

a. Shape, advance and accelerate a shared vision for empowered learning with technology by engaging with education stakeholders.

b. Advocate for equitable access to educational technology, digital content and learning opportunities to meet the diverse needs of all students.

    c. Model for colleagues the identification, exploration, evaluation, curation and adoption of new digital resources and tools for learning.

3. Citizen

Educators inspire students to positively contribute to and responsibly participate in the digital world. Educators:

    a. Create experiences for learners to make positive, socially responsible contributions and exhibit empathetic behavior online that build relationships and community.

    b. Establish a learning culture that promotes curiosity and critical examination of online resources and fosters digital literacy and media fluency.

    c. Mentor students in safe, legal and ethical practices with digital tools and the protection of intellectual rights and property.

    d. Model and promote management of personal data and digital identity and protect student data privacy.

Learning Catalyst

4. Collaborator

Educators dedicate time to collaborate with both colleagues and students to improve practice, discover and share resources and ideas, and solve problems. Educators:

    a. Dedicate planning time to collaborate with colleagues to create authentic learning experiences that leverage technology.

    b. Collaborate and co-learn with students to discover and use new digital resources and diagnose and troubleshoot technology issues.

    c. Use collaborative tools to expand students' authentic, real-world learning experiences by engaging virtually with experts, teams and students, locally and globally.

    d. Demonstrate cultural competency when communicating with students, parents and colleagues and interact with them as co-collaborators in student learning.

5. Designer

Educators design authentic, learner-driven activities and environments that recognize and accommodate learner variability. Educators:

    a. Use technology to create, adapt and personalize learning experiences that foster independent learning and accommodate learner differences and needs.

    b. Design authentic learning activities that align with content area standards and use digital tools and resources to maximize active, deep learning.

    c. Explore and apply instructional design principles to create innovative digital learning environments that engage and support learning.

6. Facilitator

Educators facilitate learning with technology to support student achievement of the 2016 ISTE Standards for Students. Educators:

    a. Foster a culture where students take ownership of their learning goals and outcomes in both independent and group settings.

    b. Manage the use of technology and student learning strategies in digital platforms, virtual environments, hands-on makerspaces or in the field.

    c. Create learning opportunities that challenge students to use a design process and computational thinking to innovate and solve problems.

    d. Model and nurture creativity and creative expression to communicate ideas, knowledge or connections.

7. Analyst

Educators understand and use data to drive their instruction and support students in achieving their learning goals. Educators:

a. Provide alternative ways for students to demonstrate competency and reflect on their learning using technology.

b. Use technology to design and implement a variety of formative and summative assessments that accommodate learner needs, provide timely feedback to students and inform instruction.

c. Use assessment data to guide progress and communicate with students, parents and education stakeholders to build student self-direction.

© 2017 International Society for Technology in Education.